Triathlon for Women

ACKNOWLEDGEMENTS

This book would not have been possible if it were not for all the women out there who have inspired me with their passion for triathlon and their support and encouragement for other women in the sport. I am forever indebted to the team of women I coached over the years in Austin, Texas. These everyday women taught me how to keep growing as a coach and kept me on my toes to learn more about the sport with all their questions and their genuine desire to become better triathletes and people.

The pages that follow flow out of my own triathlon experiences but also come from mentoring hundreds of spirited and eager women looking to engage in triathlon as a fulfilling experience for the mind, body and spirit.

Special thanks go to one of my most loyal and inspiring athletes Colleen Ryan, who really hounded me to coach her, and was always there every step of the way as we both grew in the coach-athlete relationship.

Tremendous gratitude goes out to my dedicated assistant Shellie Oroshiba, who was there throughout the entire project with ultra enthusiasm as she did research, reviewed books, provided feedback and proofread page after page, even as she prepared for her own Ironman triathlon.

I appreciate the final hour support from Cherie Gruenfeld, who wrote my final chapter and knocked me back into the writing game after I had been struggling to get to the project finish line.

Thanks also to my family who supported me even when we were on holidays at the cottage island in Georgian Bay and I had to work using solar power and wireless satellite. And of course, I thank my friends who have been there throughout all the highs and lows of my life journeys – Anna Garnett, Kathy Reesor, Julia Gerlach, Lori Campbell, and Bruce Kravitz. Last but not least, thanks as well to a few good men who have helped me through transition periods in my life with inspiration, support, or by pushing me the extra mile – Barrie Shepley, Tim Terway, Mark Lindsey, Coach Gordo, Jay Weinshenker, and Scott Messick.

Ironman Edition

Triathlon for Women

TRIATHLON

A MIND-BODY-SPIRIT APPROACH
FOR FEMALE ATHLETES

By Lisa Lynam

Published by Meyer & Meyer Sport

IRONMAN® is a registered trademark of World Triathlon Corporation

British Library Cataloguing in Publication Data
A catalogue record for this book is available from the British Library

Lisa Lynam
Triathlon for Women –
A mind-body-spirit approach for female athletes
Oxford: Meyer & Meyer Sport (UK) Ltd., 2007
ISBN 10: 1-84126-108-4
ISBN 13: 978-1-84126-108-9

© 2007 by Meyer & Meyer Sport (UK) Ltd.
Aachen, Adelaide, Auckland, Budapest, Graz, Johannesburg,
New York, Olten (CH), Oxford, Singapore, Toronto
Member of the World
Sports Publishers' Association (WSPA)
www.w-s-p-a.org
Printed and bound by: B.O.S.S Druck und Medien GmbH, Germany
ISBN 10: 1-84126-108-4
ISBN 13: 978-1-84126-108-9
E-Mail: verlag@m-m-sports.com
www.m-m-sports.com

Contents

Introduction

"Celebrate. Life is a neverending exploration of the mind, the spirit, the soul."– Monique Moore

Why read a women-only triathlon book?

Women are unique and different from men in many regards. There are obvious physical differences, and more subtle emotional and social differences. The sport of triathlon boasts tremendous gender equity, however women-only events, products and books are undeniably popular.

Beyond a score, a time on the clock or a placement on the podium, women look to their participation in sports as something special that brings strength to their lives in a holistic way. Engaging in the sport of triathlon opens the doors for women to lead healthy, happy, more fulfilled lives.

Any woman – regardless of age, color, size, or ability – whether she is an athlete or not, can embark on this three-sport journey and become empowered (in mind, body and spirit) as the special woman she is.

The goal of this book is to guide, educate and inspire women with this fulfilling mind-body-spirit approach to women's triathlon endeavors. It is my intention to impart more than just dry training theories and practical lessons, but also to foster the soul of the sport, raising the interests and enjoyment for all women who engage in a life-enhancing approach to training for triathlons, wether they be sprint or Ironman distance.

While the journey must include aspects of fitness and skill development, smart nutrition choices, strength training, race planning, and mental aspects, this book will empower real everyday women – the stay-at-home mom, the career woman, the retired woman, or any woman out there with an interest in bettering herself through triathlon.

Whether women seek to learn about getting started with triathlon life, cross the finish line of a longer distance event with a smile, or move to a higher level of excellence in triathlon racing, this book will enhance a woman's understanding of her own needs and challenges – often different from those of men – and provide guidance for her own personal triathlon journey.

Why tri? Why not?

So let's get down to the business of this book: you – the real woman – and triathlon.

If you picked up this book, you either have an interest in doing a triathlon or are already involved in training and racing and enjoy the "triathlon lifestyle." There are some women who will seek to complete just one triathlon in their lives and then there are others who will embrace the sport with passion and dedication and compete in several events. No matter your approach, there is always something to learn, some way to grow and improve yourself. This book is for every woman – to make more out her life as a result of "tri-ing."

At the end of the day, we have just one life to live, and our time on earth is precious. Indeed it's important to make the most of it. Living your life with health and happiness can get lost between all of your daily to-do lists, family obligations, and career demands. Few women will ever make a living doing triathlons, but that doesn't mean that having triathlon in your life cannot help you make a life that is more fulfilling. Thousands of women have already discovered this secret. This book will help you to think more deeply about your triathlon success and its impact on your life.

Every day we wake up with a choice: to try to live our best or not. So why try triathlon? The benefits, just a few of which I will outline below, are plentiful.

The more important question to ask might be "why not?" What fears, mental limitations or resource constraints hold you back from tri-ing or taking it to the next level? Many women cite time, money and lack of fun or support for the reasons they chose not to "tri."

Not enough time? ...money? ...fun?

Feel like you don't have enough time to pursue triathlon the way you would like to? Take a moment to consider wether there are major amounts of wasted time in your life, such as television, that you could replace with health-enhancing triathlon activities. According to the A.C. Nielsen Co., the average American watches more than 4 hours of TV each day (or 28 hour per week, or 2 months of nonstop TV-watching per year). Even just 30 minutes of swim, bike, run or strength training a day can be enough to prepare you for a short triathlon. So if you are one of the 50 percent of Americans who feel they watch too much TV, your "no time" excuse is busted.

Feel like you don't have enough money to join in on events or buy the necessary equipment? Consider that it is possible to find some great bargains on used equipment. Know also that it is ok to purchase just the basics for participation. A safe bike, helmet, running shoes, swim goggles and appropriate clothing are all it takes to start. If you have a multisport club in your area, it may organize free social training events for members. Membership benefits might also includediscounts on entry fees to local races. Check out *www.usatriathlon.org* to search for triathlon clubs in the United States.

The other benefit to being part of a club or team is that you can often find more support and potential training partners. Having someone to ride or run with (and share a few laughs and breathless moments!) can help motivate you and make the journey more enjoyable. The friends you bond with through your triathlon life will make it more fun. Some clubs may even allow you to put an ad in the club newsletter to seek training partners. You may find a club membership will allow you to connect with others at your ability level or seek out mentors to encourage you. There is also a huge online network of triathletes (such as *www.trinewbies.com*) where you can seek and share support. Local triathlon or running clubs often have chat lines or online forums as well, where new triathlon friendships are just a mouse click away. A healthy world of fun-loving triathletes awaits you!

Small steps in the journey

So what else holds you back? Perhaps it's the fear of failure? No one is asking for perfection – simply putting one foot (or arm) forward in motion is enough. You may not have the strength yet to climb the entire mountain, but starting with small steps, or taking on smaller hills, will begin the journey toward loftier heights. Why hold yourself back from the potential of enjoying the grand view at the top?

This reminds me of one of my favorite quotes from *A Return to Love* by Marianne Williamson – "We ask ourselves, 'who am I to be brilliant, gorgeous, talented, fabulous?' Actually, who are you not to be?...Your playing small doesn't serve the world. There's nothing enlightened about shrinking so that other people won't feel insecure around you.... We are all meant to shine, as children do. It's not just in some of us; it's in everyone. And as we let our own light shine, we unconsciously give other people permission to do the same."

Many women hold themselves back from doing something as apparently self-serving and self-involved as a triathlon. They often feel guilty that they may be neglecting their duties to their children, husbands, parents, community or the excessive business we can all allow our lives to be consumed by. I have always strongly believed that service to others is enhanced by our ability to first serve ourselves and fuel our own health and spirits. A flowering plant that goes without water will never be able to provide full and beautiful blossoms that others can enjoy. Nurturing your own life first with more purpose

and passionate pursuits that enhance your physical and mental fitness may seem selfish but it isnt; rather, it means you have more vitality and energy to share with those around you. You and everyone around you wins, even if you don't finish the race first.

Certainly, focused training, traveling to races, and maintenance of equipment takes time, but in the long run, a balanced approach to your triathlon endeavors will benefit not just your quality of life, but also the lives of those around you whom you love and come into contact with.

How can triathlon help women lead healthier, happier, more fulfilling lives?

Here is a list of the many benefits women can enjoy from participating in the triathlon lifestyle:

- cardiovascular fitness improvements through aerobic training make for a stronger heart muscle and vascular system with potentially lower blood pressure, lower cholesterol levels and less chance of arteriolosclerosis
- muscular fitness improvements developed through the use of a wide range of muscles used in the three different sports
- low impact cross-training reduces stress on the joints
- skill development in swimming, biking, running, strength, and flexibility
- development of endurance and stamina for physical challenges in sport or life (i.e., chasing after energetic children)
- postural stability for greater mobility as you age
- greater strength to handle labor and childbirth (really, doing a triathlon IS easier)
- mental skill development such as goal setting, focus, determination, and positive attitude
- greater confidence and sense of empowerment
- expanded knowledge of fitness and nutrition
- technical understanding of sport and sport equipment
- opportunity for social time and development of health-focused relationships

- time for solitary reflection or emotional venting
- greater sense of self and independence
- greater sense of achievement or satisfaction
- becoming a positive role model for family, friends and children
- possibility to become a mentor or coach and inspire others
- opportunity for community involvement and contribution
- opportunity to explore new roads, trails or venture closer to nature
- opportunity to travel to new places and experience new cultures for races
- opportunity for self actualization of ultimate life goals or potential
- opportunity to explore your physical limits
- opportunity to have a ton of fun!!!

Few activities can offer so many benefits like triathlon can to women of every ability and age. These are a few of the mind-body-spirit benefits most women can gain from the sport. Incorporated into your life in a balanced, healthy way, triathlon can help empower you to believe *anything is possible*! Consider writing down a few benefits to post on your fridge or on a card in your office when you need some extra motivation as to why you tri.

Triathlon can provide each woman with a unique gift that makes life more special. Not everyone will become consumed by the triathlon lifestyle, nor will they desire to. Still, I hope each woman who reads this book considers what gifts this swim-bike-run sport can bring to her life beyond just the physical benefits. Ultimately, a worthy recreational pursuit should be fun and life enhancing to our physical, mental, emotional, social and spiritual well being.

If you are a triathlon veteran, it might be useful to write down a few of your thoughts on how triathlon has affected your life before you proceed with the rest of the book. You can then add to the list as you progress in your journey. Your enjoyment of the sport will likely be enhanced from simply reminding yourself what to be grateful for when you head out for your next arduous workout.

The challenges of triathlon aren't easy by any means, but rarely is any worthwhile endeavor easy.

The good news is that women have several attributes that make them particularly well suited to succeed in multisport. Consider how well women multitask and organize multiple roles. Juggling multiple sports into their lives comes naturally. Women tend to take their time developing a safe and sensible plan and follow directions with discipline and patience. Women also value the emotional satisfaction and social bonds more often than men, who tend to chase endless records and competitive challenges. This is not to say that women can't be competitive, and certainly victory is a great emotional reward, but women are good at keeping sport in perspective.

Make the leap with Triathlon for Women

If you are hesitant about making the leap to do your first triathlon, are not sure what you need to work on or what training directions you might take, or are struggling to improve your overall enjoyment in the sport, this book will provide you with guidance.

Part One helps you **Get It Together** by preparing your mind and discussing the equipment and clothing best for women. Part Two helps you **Get Moving** by introducing fitness basics and discussing women's differences in sport physiology (such as the impact of hormones and the menstrual cycle on performance).

Part Two offers a plethora of drills and tips to practice, practice, practice to perfect your skills in swim, bike and run. Differences in the female body and their impact on technique are also discussed. This section also includes a closer look at mental skills, with an emphasis on those skills that women need the most.

Part Three urges you to **Get Involved** by showing you how to become part of the triathlon community, build friendships, find training partners and seek out social opportunities to enhance your enjoyment. Part Three also discusses coaching aspects – how to find a coach and make the best of a coaching relationship, as well as how to become involved in mentoring or coaching others when you feel ready to share your gifts.

Part Four provides advice on how to **Get Training** by helping you to put together or find a plan right for you and directing you to available resources. Part Four also includes nutrition advice and a discussion on women's specific nutritional issues as they relate to triathlon. This section also contains healthy recipes for busy women looking to keep energized before, during and after training. Part Four finishes with race planning details, providing all-important checklists to keep you organized, as well as providing travel and triathlon vacation considerations.

The book concludes with Part Five, **Get Balanced**, which presents key tips for keeping your sanity while balancing life and triathlon, and delves more deeply into specific challenges for women, such as childcare, menopause, and safety.

If you need a boost of inspiration, read the stories throughout this book about real women like you with busy lives who have integrated triathlon into their lives in positive ways.

CHAPTER 1

History of Women in Triathlon

In the beginning...

Women have not always competed in sport competitions as they do today. The first Olympics in 776 B.C. excluded women, so they assembled for their own Games of Hera, which honored the Greek goddess who ruled over women and the earth. Thankfully, women today are free to participate in sport in most, but still not all, countries around the world.

Just before the turn of the 20th century women found a sense of freedom and mobility in bicycling – over one quarter of all new bicycles purchased then were by women. As Susan B. Anthony said "the bicycle has done more for the emancipation of women than anything else in the world."

Up until 1968, women were not allowed to run in the Boston Marathon because it was believed such endurance events were too strenuous for women. It took the courage of Kathrine Switzer, who entered the 1967 race as K. Switzer to change this view. An attempt by a race official to throw her off the course was thwarted by her boyfriend who was running the course with her. This incident ignited the women's running revolution in the '70s. Switzer went on to run another 35 marathons and initiate the Avon International Running Circuit, a global series of women's running events in 25 countries, involving over one million women. With the help of Switzer's lobbying, the women's marathon was finally included in the 1984 Olympic Games.

Enthusiasm for women's running trickled into triathlon when the triple-sport began to take off in the 1970s. Women were welcomed to participate equally from the early days of triathlon. Men and women compete over the same distance and course, unlike in other sports, such as cycling, where women have limited and shorter events to participate in.

The first triathlon known, the Mission Bay Triathlon, took place in 1974. It wasn't until the 1982 Ironman Hawaii event, however, when ABC Sports captured a crawling Julie Moss at the finish line, that triathlon and women's participation began to take off. The year 1982 also marked the first all-women's triathlon, sponsored by Bonnie Bell cosmetics, at Marine World Africa USA.

Throughout the '80s and early '90s, women's participation at the Ironman Hawaii grew until the percentage hovered around 20 percent (see Table 1). Women were also joining USA Triathlon, the governing body of triathlon in the U.S. in similar percentages at the same time. (See Table 3). The most recent membership report indicates a steady growth of women in the sport, with women comprising one third of USAT members. With over 16,000 women belonging to the national governing body in America, women are clearly embracing the sport.

Emergence of Danskin butterflies

Women's participation in triathlon received a huge boost at the grass roots level with the introduction of the Danskin Women's Triathlon Series in 1990. The immensely successful series that began with only three races and 150 entrants produced its 100th race in 2005 as part of the eight-race series in prominent U.S. cities. In 2004, four Danskin events ranked among the 10 largest races nationwide in the U.S. with over 2,500 participants (see Table 4).

According to Danskin, by 2005 over 140,000 women had crossed the finish line under the Danskin banner and created a new culture where everyday women, many with no previous athletic experience, were transformed from "caterpillars into butterflies." The Danskin finisher's medal slogan, "The woman who starts the race is not the same as the woman who finishes it," has sparked the desire of thousands of women to continue to swim, bike, run for fitness, fun and competition.

Women's triathlon icon Sally Edwards took the lead as the Danskin series spokeswoman and ensured that women could participate without the intimidation often felt in mixed (gender) events. Edwards even guaranteed that no woman would ever have to fear finishing last as she can be found at the back of the pack and is the official final finisher at every event.

Sally's encouragement and pre-race clinics have certainly been instrumental in gaining more universal participation by women in the sport. "Every woman is capable of completing a triathlon – every size, every shape, every age," says Edwards in her book *Triathlons for Women*.

The Danskin series isn't the only women-only series to note. In 1995, Canadian age-group triathlete Tina Braam put on an all-women's race in her hometown Milton, Ontario, just west of Toronto. Since then, the event has grown to be part of the Ontario Women's Triathlon Series, with three events and pre-race clinics. The race is also part of the National series of women's triathlons now produced across Canada. (See Table 5 for race info.)

The Reebok Women's Triathlon Series recently started with four events in major U.S. cities. The Naperville, Illinois (Chicago) event was ranked as the 16th largest triathlon in the U.S. The Nike Women's Triathlon series started with two events in Vancouver, Washington and Sacramento, California, with those two women-only events now independently managed by PM Events and TBF Racing respectively.

A number of individual all-women's events have spotted the triathlon calendars over the years, the most notable of which is the Women's Gold Nugget Triathlon in Anchorage, Alaska, beginning in 1984. What began as a way for event directors to do the sport with their daughters has become the longest-standing women's event still running today, with over 800 women participating each May. A phenomenal feat considering the less-than-ideal triathlon conditions in Alaska!

Women's events have seemed to sprout up anywhere there is a woman or group eager to get women into the sport. Beyond the large city stops on the Danskin tour, women-only races currently exist in other locations, such as Sugarland (Houston, Texas), Ohio, Hawaii, and even Cancun, Mexico. The year 2005 marked the first Isla Mujeres Triathlon in Cancun (*www.sportscancun.com*). Barb's Race is the world's only Half-Ironman distance event held on the same day and course as the Vineman full distance in Santa Rosa, California. Since 2000, Barb's Race has been held in honor of Barbara Recchia, a long-time Vineman volunteer and race committee member who has twice been faced with the daunting task of fighting cancer, and still lives today (*www.vineman.com*). Check out *www.hertri.info* for the current calendar of women's races around the world.

Women's presence at the Ironman distance

What began in 1978 as a contest of 15 men competing in the toughest Hawaiian endurance race to claim the name "Ironman," has grown to include some of the world's best female professional and age-group athletes testing their physical and mental stamina to earn the title of Ironman. The epic endurance event comprising a 3.8km swim, 180 km bike ride followed by a 42.2 km marathon run (or 2.4 mile swim, 112 mile bike, and 26.2 mile run) is now known as the World Ironman Championships. Despite the title "Ironman" and its start with just men in the field, the event has grown to attract more and more women.

In its first three years (1978-1980) there were zero, one and two women entered in the race in each respective year. Women's participation grew considerably in the late 1980s, when the field of women grew to a high of 266 participants or 20.9 percent of the field in 1988 (see Table 1). In more recent years, the field at the Ironman World Championships has included 350 or so women, which is still roughly 20 percent of the field.

When Ironman events hit continental America around the year 2000, women filled up at least a fifth of the entry slots (see Table 2). By 2005, more and more women were finding their way to an Ironman start line, many who likely began with the Danskin races and were ready for a bigger challenge. Women accounted for one quarter of the participants at most Ironman North America events in 2005. The largest number of female competitors ever in an Ironman – 738 or 30.4 percent of the field – was recorded at Ironman Canada 2005.

The message is loud and clear that women too are raising their arms at the finish line to claim "I am an Ironman!"

Triathlon women on the world stage

In 2000, the profile of women in triathlon received a global injection. The summer Olympics in Sydney opened with the inaugural women's triathlon event and world-wide broadcasters showcased the world's best female triathletes swimming, biking and running for more than two hours in the quest for Olympic glory. Switzerland's Brigitte McMahon out-sprinted World Champion Michellie Jones, of Australia, by just two seconds to win gold and imprint a sensational picture of women's triathlon in the minds of millions of viewers worldwide.

The Athens Olympics garnered even more media attention. According to Nielson Media Research, 24.3 million households viewed the NBC prime time coverage for the women's triathlon and was the third most watched show for the week. Outdoor Life Network regularly covers ITW World Cup events and Ironman races with women competitors receiving equal attention.

Today the numbers of women participating in the sport have continued to grow. According to statistics collected by USA Triathlon, in the early 1980s less than ten percent of its members were women. By 2000, the percentage grew to 27.4 percent, and by 2004, 34 percent of the membership were women – 16,409 women in all (Table 3). That number doesn't include the one-day memberships or other women doing triathlon without annual USAT memberships. Women aged thirty to forty-nine are the largest age group within the USA Triathlon membership. The numbers decline heavily for women in their fifties (Table 6).

The rising equality of professional women in triathlon

Also noteworthy in the 2004 USAT demographics report is that 39 percent of the total number of elite professionals registered with USA Triathlon are female. The barriers for U.S. women to take on professional triathlon as a career have fallen, especially with the recent success of women role models like 2004 World Champion Sheila Taormina, World Cup contender Barb Lindquist, and Olympian Joanna Zeiger. The percentage of professional women is somewhat surprising considering many women sacrifice their professional careers for childbirth and raising a family.

Perhaps this figure is evidence of the expanding opportunities for both male and female triathletes alike, or more support for women to pursue professional triathlon careers. Lobbying by committees such as the ITU (International Triathlon Union) Women's Commission since its inception in 1990 by Sarah Springman, of Great Britain, and Lori Cameron, of Australia, has helped equalize prize money and media opportunities in the international racing field.

The ultimate in equalizing opportunities appeared for women in 2002 with the development of the Lifetime Fitness Triathlon in Minneapolis, Minnesota. An "Equalizer" format allowed women and men to race each other for the top prize – a $250,000 check. "The women get a head start but the chivalry ends there," is the race slogan. The professional women receive a slight head start, as determined by previous year's results and the personal records of the professionals participating, and the first man or woman across the line wins the overall prize. American Barb Lindquist won in 2002 and 2003, and Australian Loretta Harrop in 2004, before the boys could even the score 3-1 with Craig Alexander taking the top prize in 2005. The best female of the day, 2003 World Champion Emma Snowsill, still took away $80,000 and a $40,000 vehicle for her top performance.

Certainly, female professionals in the sport are enjoying more financial opportunities and equal media coverage. We've come a long way, baby!

Beyond the racing course, women have found their way into more leadership positions in the sport, as well. Race director Valerie Silk is well known for founding and elevating the Ironman Hawaii event to its current prominence in the media. Sarah Springman served as the Vice President of the ITU from 1992-96 and was instrumental in the formative years of the sport on the Olympic stage. Gale Bernhart served as the first female coach for the U.S. Olympic triathlon team in 2004.

Table 1
Women Participants in Ironman World Championships early years (Source: Triathlete Magazine)

Year	Starters Women	Finishers Women	Starters Total	Percentage of Total Starters
1978	0	0	15	0.0%
1979	1	1	15	6.7%
1980	2	2	108	1.9%
1981	20	16	326	6.1%
1982	49	47	580	8.4%
1982	92	85	850	10.8%
1985	189	173	1018	18.6%
1988	266	240	1275	20.9%
1990	257	223	1387	18.5%
1991	264	249	1379	19.1%
1992	273	261	1364	20.0%

Table 2
Women Participation in Ironman North America events 2000 and 2005 (Source: Ironman North America)

Event	2000		2004	
	Women in field	Total numbers	Women in field	Total numbers
Ironman Arizona	NA	NA	445 (20.79%)	2140
California Half	519 (25.44%)	2040	625 (26.13%)	2392
Florida Half	NA	NA	563 (25.6%)	2199
Ironman Couer D'Alene	492 (24.14%)	2038	399 (20.76%)	1922
Ironman USA	449 (21.77%)	2062	497 (22.62%)	2198
Ironman Canada	604 (28.24%))	2139	738 (30.37%)	2430
Ironman Wisconsin	402 (20.43%)	1968	539 (24.07%)	2239

Table 3
USA Triathlon Annual Member History By Gender
(Source: USAT Demographics report, 2005)

	1986	1994	Aug 2000	Sep 2001	Dec 2003	Dec 2004
Male	78%	82%	19,360 72.7%	21,496 71.4%	32,290 68%	35,252 66%
Female	22%	19%	7,242 27.3%	8,605 28.6%	15,083 32%	16,409 34%
Total	approx 5,000	approx 15,000	26,602	30,101	47,373	53,254

Table 4
Top USA Triathlon-Sanctioned Races in 2004 by Age-Group Participation
(Source: USAT Demographics report, 2005)

Event	Participants
#1 Accenture Chicago Triathlon (Ill.)*	4,953
#2 Wildflower (Calif.)*	4,786
#3 St. Anthony's Triathlon (Fla.)*	2,999
#4 Danskin-Wisconsin	2,825
#5 Danskin-Seattle	2,627
#6 Danskin-Austin	2,576
#7 Danskin-Denver	2,504
#16 Reebok Women's Tri-Naperville (Ill.)	1,636

Table 5
All women's races

Series:

Danskin Women's Triathlon Series	(www.danskin.com/triathlon.html)
Reebok Women's Triathlon Series	(www.reebokwomentriathlon.com)
Canada National Women's Series	
Kincardine Triathlon	(www.kincardinetriathlon.com)
Saskatoon Just Tri It	(www.justtri-it.com)
Hampton, New Brunswick	(jmross@nb.sympatico.ca)
Regina Multisport	(www.reginamultisport.com)
Strathmore Triathlon	(www.leapingdogracing.com)
Vancouver Triathlon	(www.reflexionclinics.com)
Sorel-Tracy, Quebec	(www.triathlonquebec.org)
Ontario Women's Triathlon Series	(www.womenstriathlon.com)

    Orangeville
    Grimsby
    Milton

Other women's triathlons

Barb's Race (Half-Iron distance on Vineman course), Santa Rosa, CA	(www.vineman.com)
Luna Bar All Women's Triathlon, Sacramento, CA	(www.tbfracing.com)
Vancouver Women's Triathlon, Vancouver, WA	(www.pmevents.com)
Luna All Women's Triathlon, Oregon	(www.racecenter.com/allwomens)
Speedo Women's Triathlon, Sugarland (Houston), TX	
Women's Gold Nugget Triathlon, Anchorage, AK	(www.goldnuggettriathlon.com)
Women-only Triathlon, Ohio	(www.hfpracing.com)
Girl Power Triathlon, New Orleans, LA	(www.girlpowertri.com)
City of Philadelphia Women's Triathlon	(www.cgiraing.com)
Isla Mujeres Triathlon Women Only, Cancun, Mexico	(www.sportscancun.com)
Tough Cookie Duathlon, Austin, TX	(www.tcdcfitness.com)
Power Maiden Triathlon, Athens, TX	(www.ironheadrp.com)

(See www.trifind.com for a more complete, current list of all races for women)

Table 6
Breakdown of 2004 annual membership per age group
(Numbers are approximate)
(Source: USA Triathlon Demographics report, 2005)

Age-group	Female	% of age-group	Male	% of age-group	Total in age-group	% in relation to all current members
Under 16	326	43%	425	57%	751	1.4%
16-19	237	36%	426	64%	663	1.2%
20-29	3,403	43%	4,485	57%	7,888	15%
30-39	6,512	32%	13,595	68%	20,107	38%
40-49	4,315	29%	10,367	71%	14,682	28%
50-59	1,215	23%	4,079	77%	5,294	9.9%
60-69	216	16%	1,115	84%	1,331	2.5%
70-79	28	15%	163	85%	191	0.4%
80-plus	0		15	100%	15	

PART 1
Get It Together

CHAPTER 2

Preparing Your Mind

The most important thing you can do when starting out or considering how to improve is to **prepare**. Good preparation includes preparing a **plan**. But there is something even more primary and essential to the process of getting the most out of your triathlon endeavors – preparing **your mind**.

It is often said that where the mind goes, the body follows. If you have not made the commitment in your mind, no amount of talent, no perfect plan, no coach, no training partner will get you to do the work necessary to reap success. This is often the first place that women will limit themselves – in their minds. When the topic of triathlon comes up, I frequently hear "I could never do that!" or "I don't know how to do that!"

Barring some genetic limitations or financial constraints, your limits will be only those that you create in your mind. Take a moment to consider how you might be limiting your triathlon success with your mind. What might you dare to do or dream about achieving if there was no chance of failure or risk of ridicule? Is an Ironman distance triathlon really out of reach? Are you able to put one foot in front of the other? Is a new PR or winning that local race really that impossible? Stop and ask, **why not?**

That said, everyone has various obstacles or challenges that can hold them back from achieving their goals. There are realities to time and resource constraints, especially for women with children and full-time jobs. Still, almost any obstacle or challenge can be overcome with the right **attitude**. I hear non-triathlon women say things like "my knees are bad, so I can't run" or "I don't have enough money for a bike" or "I'm afraid of open water swimming." Not one of these excuses is bound to stop someone who truly puts her mind to the challenge and diligently practices with the discipline necessary to succeed.

One of my athletes Carol could not run due to a bone problem in her foot, despite several surgeries. What she could do was put one foot in front of the other to walk swiftly and keep a relentless positive attitude. She finished the Danskin Triathlon in 2002, then went on to walk a half marathon, and recently finished a Half-Ironman distance triathlon in under the cut-off time of 8 hours. It was a huge personal victory for Carol. Her disability did not hinder her mind. She reaped the rewards of the journey and the fantastic feeling at the finish line. She had completed something many would have thought was out of reach given her disability. Don't let your mind be your disability. Try the magic words "Why Not?" more often!

The recipe for preparing your mind for overcoming obstacles

The key toward overcoming any obstacle is to first believe. Next, commit in your mind to making the steps forward, toward your goal. Finally, persevere when the going gets tough.

Believe. Commit. Persevere. Repeat.

Consider the obstacles for Sarah Reinertsen in becoming the first woman amputee to finish the prestigious Ironman World Championships in Hawaii in 2005. In her first attempt (2004), on a very tough, windy day she missed the bike cut-off time and was not allowed to continue after already having put in 10 hours of effort in her race. Her tears of sadness turned to joy a year later when she persevered and returned to Hawaii to successfully finish the Ironman World Championship triathlon! Reinertsen prepared her mind with the "believe, commit, persevere" recipe and reaped personal victory.

Even the very best professional triathlon women face obstacles that may have once seemed insurmountable. Take Karen Smyers, three-time ITU World Champion (1990, 1995 short course, 1996 long course) and 1995 Ironman World Champion, as an example. After some challenging years that included recovering from thyroid cancer treatments, a broken collar bone, a C-section and 48 hours of labor, an accident with an 18-wheeler and a storm window slicing her hamstring, Smyers kept her attitude focused on simply being happy to be running and biking again, period.

"After you get hit, you have to pick yourself back up from square one. The important thing for me is to not look back too often and get too discouraged about where I was," said Smyers, at age 39, while recovering in 2001. Her perseverance and attitude has allowed her to continue to be one of the world's best female triathletes even into her mid-forties.

"Just think about the little steps in your progress," suggested Smyers. "Start from where you are and as long as you are moving forward, you are eventually going to climb pretty high. It isn't easy. I've definitely had those days when I've had a swim workout that was particularly depressing where I'm wondering if I'll ever get back to where I was. Usually it's temporary."

"It's also helped me to read books like Lance Armstrong's book. It's kept things in perspective for me. As bad as I've felt I've had it at times, I've had a pretty charmed existence and have so many great things going for me."

Age group women (those who race as amateurs categorized by age, usually by five year age groups) like 53-year-old Linda Quirk, had her perseverance tested in 2005. An almost fatal accident on her bike left the grandmother with a fractured skull, but her mind was still strong, and she went on to qualify for the Long Course Worlds and the Ironman World Championshps. Read more about Linda's story and comeback attitude below.

Linda Quirk: Mind over Matter

Last year, I thought my triathlon experiences were over due to an almost fatal bike accident. I managed to make it to the Long Course Worlds in Sweden, four months after the accident, and finished in a respectable 9th place.

I was riding the Solvang Century (something I had done twice before) in California when I believe while coming down a hill my front wheel hit a pothole. I don't remember much of the accident, but my coach turned around to see me, as he put it, torpedo head first into the ground going about 25 mph. I fractured just about every bone in my head including the bones around the eyes. I spent three days in ICU and four more days in a Santa Barbara hospital before flying back to our new home in Florida to be seen by a neurologist at the Mayo Clinic. My husband and children, as well as my coach and friends, were my constant support.

Returning to triathlon and riding again was a challenge that I knew I had to pursue. With a lot of patience and determination I realized that everything does happen for a reason. My resolve to make it to the Long Course Worlds last year was the turning point where I knew that I could conquer my fears.

When I successfully qualified for Kona at Ironman Lanzarote, it was not only exciting for me but also for my children and grandchildren to see that perseverance and hard work can only lead to success. As I have always told them, if you can "see it" you can do it and if you "believe it," it will happen!

Assessment – Health, fitness and performance

Before your goals are developed, it is important to assess where you currently stand in the areas of health, fitness and performance; then use this assessment as a beginning benchmark to see how you are progressing as you take steps toward meeting your goals.

1. **What is your overall health and wellness like?**
   Give yourself a score for your health and wellness (1-10): (1 poor to 10 excellent) _____ (review this score in six months or periodically)

   ⮞ Health and wellness can be defined as a state of living without disease and with an enhanced quality of life through positive lifestyle behaviors and attitudes.

2. **What is your overall level of fitness currently?**
   Give yourself a score for your fitness based on the physiological factors below (1-10):(1 poor to 10 excellent) _____ (review this score in six months or periodically)

   ⮞ Fitness is an improved physiological state that leads to improved health and longevity. Fitness can be assessed by the following components:
   i. cardiovascular – respiration, circulation, cardiac output
   ii. muscular – lean body mass
   iii. flexibility – range of motion of joints
   iv. body composition – proportion of fat-free mass (bone, muscle, blood, organs, fluids) – to fat mass (adipose tissue deposited under skin and around organs)
   v. other fitness aspects – balance, coordination, speed, power, mental capability

3. **What level of performance are you currently capable of?**
   Give yourself a score for your recent performances in sport (1-10): (1 poor to 10 excellent) _____ (review this score pre- and post- season)

   ⮞ Performance is defined as the execution of a sport or activity with a high degree of synergy of mind and body.

Beyond a self-assessment of your health, fitness and performance, an annual physical or health check is important. Of particular importance to women are assessments of iron and HDL levels and female specific health issues (i.e., breast exam, pap smear).

Assessment – Understand your strengths and weaknesses

In order to succeed in reaching your goals – whatever your aim – you will benefit from understanding your current position and the challenges before you.

An overall basic assessment of where you are with regard to your health, fitness and performance, as reviewed above, is a good starting point.

To develop your body for triathlon, consider a more specific assessment of your strengths and weaknesses relating to the demands of triathlon. For instance, physical endurance, mental concentration, emotional patience, and social confidence will enhance your ability to succeed in and enjoy your triathlon endeavors. Take a moment to note your strengths in each area that you believe will help you succeed and your weaknesses that you will need to work toward overcoming in the chart on the following page.

Assessment of Your Strengths and Weaknesses for Triathlon Training and Racing

Assessment area	Strengths	Weaknesses
Physical		
Mental (concentration, confidence, race strategy, visualization)		
Emotional (passion, stability, patience)		
Spiritual (faith, trust)		
Social/relationships		
Resources		

Goal setting

Once you understand your position of health and fitness, the strengths and weaknesses you possess, and the challenges you face, you can set meaningful, effective goals. A goal is defined as a positive motivational strategy to enhance performance by focusing attention and promoting increased persistence (USAT coaching manual, 2000).

Why set goals?
- Clarify expectations
- Create intrinsic motivation
- Develop performance satisfaction when goals are executed
- Enhance attention and focus on tasks in line with goals
- Enhance strategy development
- Foster discipline and effort
- Encourage persistence with clear vision of direction and aims

Goal-setting success involves goals that are:
1. Positive
2. **Process oriented** – focusing on your own performance, such as learning lessons and improvements, not outcomes is the best approach. Setting a goal for a certain time or placing other goals that are impacted by factors outside your control are difficult to evaluate if the weather is bad or the field is stacked with top-level competition.
3. **Achievable, but challenging** – if the goal is too easy it will not motivate you appropriately, but if it is too out of reach it may become too discouraging. Still, shooting for the stars, and landing on the moon is a healthy way to look at setting far-fetched goals.
4. **Personal** – your goals, not someone else's. When the obstacles build, it will be your own deep personal passion that prevails.
5. **Specific and measurable** – if the goal is too vague, there will be no deadline to work toward with a sense of healthy urgency. Set a date to achieve the goal and a way to evaluate your successful achievement of the goal, such as a measurable time, an improvement percentage, or a checklist of skills developed. That way you will be able to set the date of your victory party, too!
6. **Short term, medium term and long term** – give thought to this season, next year and beyond, and reflect on the small goals you will need to reach in the short term for your bigger long-term goals. Completing an Ironman triathlon three years down the road is a longterm goal that is supported by planning shorter-term goals, such as completing an Olympic distance this season, and medium-term goals, such as finishing a Half-Ironman (70.3) distance or a century (100 mile) bike ride next season.

Common mistakes made when setting goals:
- Too many
- Too general
- Failure to support with enough time and resources
- Failure to evaluate
- Failure to modify
- Setting outcome vs. performance or process goals

Consider setting goals not just for the obvious, like a faster time, but other aspects of your physical, mental, emotional, social, spiritual, and financial health. A race goal I've found particularly rewarding over the years has been to meet three new people or give a compliment or positive word of encouragement to everyone I talk to. Trophies and medals bring little but dust later on, but expanding my fellowship with other athletes I respect keeps my social life glowing. A well-rounded mind-body-spirit approach to triathlon goals will enhance your chances of enjoying triathlon and having a more fulfilling life.

Take a moment below to write down three short-term goals for your next triathlon season. Focus on the successful completion of an event, the development of a skill, or the introduction of a process for your triathlon season following the six goal-setting success guidelines listed previously. Consider the various race distances in Table 7.

Short-term goals for this season:
1.
_____

2.
_____

3.
_____

RACE FORMATS	DISTANCES (SWIM/BIKE/RUN)*
Super Sprint	Swim 375 m/Bike 10 km/Run 2.5 km
Sprint	Swim 750 m/Bike 20K/Run 5K
Olympic	Swim 1.5 km/Bike 40 km/Run 10 km
Half-Ironman/70.3 distance	Swim 1.9 km/ Bike 90 km/Run 21 km
ITU Long course (Nice distance)	Swim 4 km/Bike 120 km/Run 30km
Ironman or Ultra distance	Swim 3.8 km/Bike 180 km/Run 42 km

Other distances:
Ultraman, Double Ironman, Triple Ironman or Deca Ironman (10 times the distance!)

Note: The distances in each classification can sometimes vary with some races, having longer bike distance or shorter swims. This is often due to the need to fit a course to the environment.

CHAPTER 3
Equipment Essentials

Shopping for equipment and clothing to get started

It's time to suit up and get the equipment that will enable you to get going in the swim, bike and run.

But first, there are some very important things to remember – never sacrifice comfort or safety for dollar savings. A few more dollars spent to get the equipment right for you will alleviate potential suffering, injuries or lack of enjoyment. The more you can be comfortable while pursuing your sport, the more you will be successful.

Also, keep in mind that what is right for your body and fitness will change over the years as you continue to train. When I started running, I began with shoes to correct for over-pronation and avoid injury. Now, however, I can wear almost any type of shoe, including racing flats with little support, and be fine. It took years to develop a stronger foot and biomechanical support within my body – stronger muscles, connective tissues and more effective biomechanics.

Do your research and get more than one person's or salesperson's opinion on your potential purchases. Try to discern what is truly best for you, your situation and your goals. Someone who is new to triathlon and 30 lbs overweight is not going to be best suited on a tri position bike, yet I see dealers put women in this situation frequently. Consider talking to other athletes for their advice or experience with a product you are considering to purchase. Don't feel rushed to buy anything, especially big ticket items like a bike, as you may regret it later if you don't take the time to gather information and test a number of comparable products. Always walk away feeling like you made an informed choice that is best for your situation.

Have an idea of **your budget** before you hit the stores. Do some **comparison shopping** and negotiate the final **deal** on big purchases like bikes. The remainder of the chapter will discuss the various items you should consider for your triathlon endeavors. Once you have a good idea of your individual needs try using the Shopping List table below to organize your shopping activities and keep track of your findings.

Shopping Tips Summary
- Never sacrifice comfort or safety
- Do your research
- Know your budget
- Comparison shop
- Negotiate deals

Shopping List

Item	Store or online shop	Priority	Price	Comments
Swim				
Bike				
Run				
Accessories				

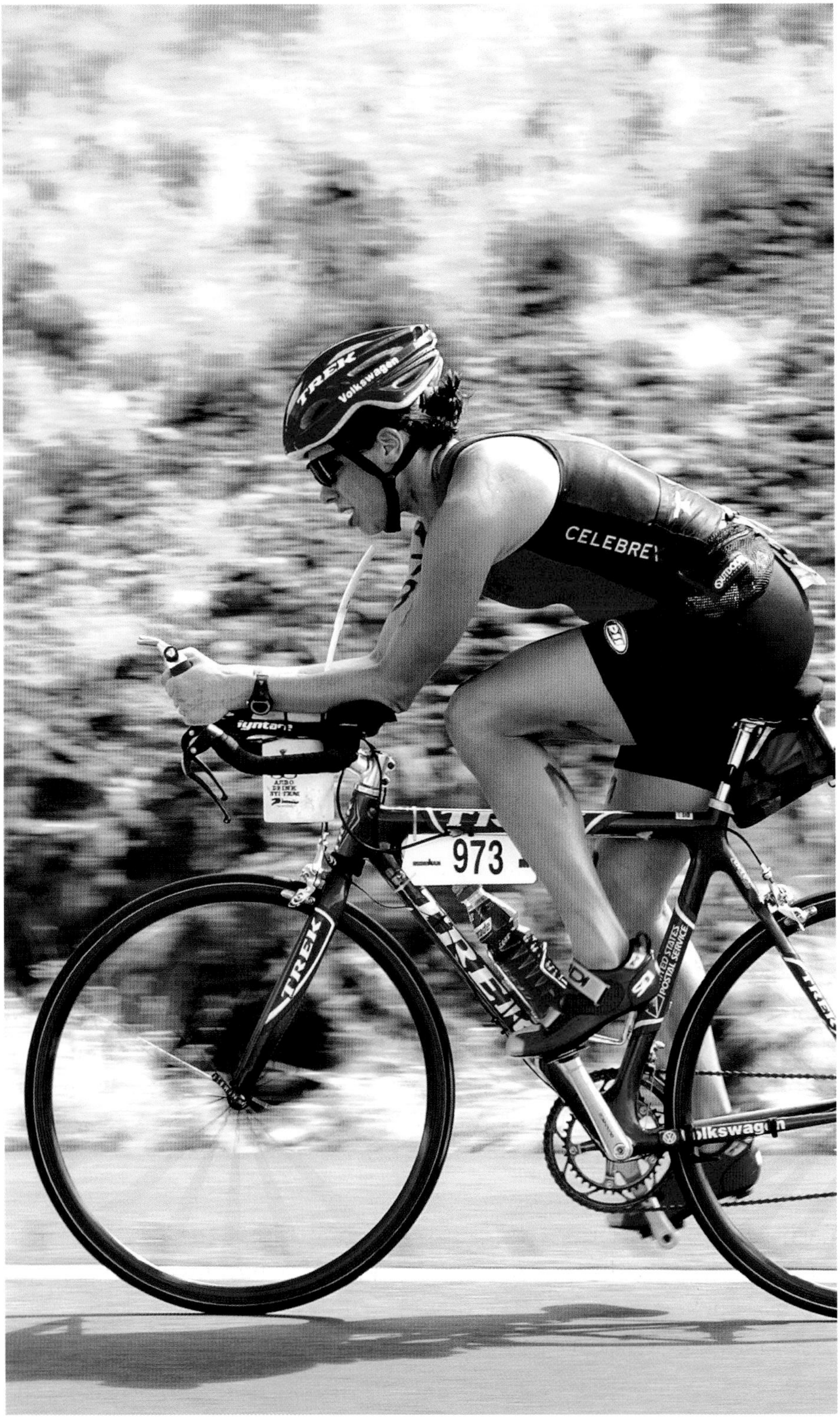
TREK
Volkswagen
CELEBREX
973
TREK
Volkswagen

Essentials for the starting tri woman: Basic training equipment

Getting together all the items you need, or think you need, as a triathlon woman can be a daunting task. But like the race itself, consider taking one step at a time, starting with the basics. When it comes down to it, you can participate in triathlon training and racing with a few key items: a swimsuit and goggles, a safe bike and helmet, and running shoes, plus appropriate clothing for the weather.

Guidelines on what to consider in your search for each of these basic equipment needs are outlined below.

SWIM

Swimsuit – Lycra suits can be purchased at sports stores or online at swim specialty stores. Make sure you can get ample movement of the arms. Try a few arm rotations and mimic the swim stroke to make sure the suit is not too tight, will ride up the butt or dig into your shoulders and back. The materials should prevent chafing. Pay special attention to seams as they can chafe too.

Know that lycra material will also deteriorate rather quickly in chlorine, especially if you like to wear it in hot tubs. Look for swimsuits that are "chlorine resistant." Also, make sure you rinse and dry your suit well after each use to prolong its life.

Goggles – The most important purpose of the swim goggles is to protect your eyes and allow you to see where you are swimming. You don't want to go swimming and end up with red stinging eyes because chlorinated water got into your goggles. So don't skimp on price with these if it means having irritated eyes, leaky goggles, frequent fogging or poor fit.

Each woman will find there is a shape and brand that fits her most comfortably. Test the goggles out in the store by pressing them into the eye sockets and seeing if they fit. Lift your eyebrows up first and press into eye sockets. Each side of the goggle should stick for a few seconds.

Goggles should also have lenses with UV protection, and possibly reflective shades, for outdoor swimming or racing in the sun.

If you find your goggles fog up easily in the environment you are swimming in, buy anti-fog goggles, purchase defogging solution to use on the inside of the lenses, or try rubbing some saliva on the lenses.

A lot of women worry about wearing their contacts while swimming. In my 14 years of triathlon, I have never had a problem with wearing my contacts while using goggles for swimming and racing. If the goggles come off during a race, you may have to close your eyes, but I've never lost a contact.

BIKE

Cycling is the sport that involves the most equipment purchases. Although it is a little more complex, women should not feel intimidated. You can build your knowledge and experience with bike equipment. I take pride in my ability to handle my bike equipment and know this builds my confidence and enjoyment for the cycling part of triathlon.

A typical bike is made up of a **frame, a fork, wheels, components and other add-on accessories**. When you purchase a bike in stock in a local bike shop, you will be getting it already assembled with all but the add-on accessories, such as aerobars, odometer, power meter and possibly clipless pedals.

The frame can be manufactured out of a number of different materials: carbon, aluminum, titanium, steel tubing, or a mix of these materials. Each material has its advantages, disadvantages and price. Generally, steel is the least expensive and best buy for entry-level bikes. If budget is not a limitation, then the choice of a carbon, aluminum or titanium frame are better options. Aluminum is very stiff, and the vibration can be hard on the bodies of smaller women, so carbon or titanium often provide a more comfortable ride. Most forks, which hold the front wheel in place, are carbon as it will absorb vibrations from the road and provide better comfort. Carbon is also a lot lighter material, so a carbon fork will contribute to decreasing the weight of your bike.

In recent years, more manufacturers have created women's frames that are not just smaller versions of men's frames, but adjusted to a woman's body. Trek, Cannondale and Terry are a few of the companies that market specific women's designs with shorter top tubes and other women friendly parts like narrower handlebars and smaller shifters for a woman's smaller hands.

When looking for a used bike, consider it to be like a car purchase and ask a lot of questions. If the bike is used, ask if it has ever been in an accident and why the person is selling it. It is worth the expense to take a used bike to a bike mechanic to evaluate it.

Road bike vs. triathlon bike

A common consideration for many women in triathlon will be whether they should purchase a road bike or a triathlon bike. What is the difference you ask?

As Hazen Kent explains in his article on Tri-Newbies Online, "The major difference between the triathlon bike and the traditional road bike lies in the geometry of the bicycle frame. Specifically, I am referring to the seat tube angle. The seat tube is the long tube extending from the bottom bracket upward towards the seat. And the angle of this tube relative to a horizontal line drawn at the bottom bracket represents your seat tube angle."

The seat tube angle for a triathlon bike is usually 76 to 78 degrees, which is steeper than the 72-degree angle found on most road bikes. The tri-bike angle puts the rider in a more forward position and this results in a better aerodynamic position.

The forward position is not only more aerodynamic, but also less demanding on the quadriceps muscles. This can help save your legs for the run.

Road bikes can become more like a tri bike by turning the seat post around to put the rider more forward.

Bike fits for different bodies

Since every woman's body is a little different in her dimensions, strength and flexibility, your bike needs to be set up uniquely for your body in order to get the most comfort, power and efficiency.

A bike "fitting" can be done at your local bike dealer, by following advice in a book, such as *The Female Cyclist* by Gale Bernhardt, or by following the detailed advice on Dan Empfield's web site at www.slowtwitch.com. Some shops will have a professional fitter or use a Fit Kit at a reasonable cost to get you properly set up for your anatomy and fitness. This book does not get into the full guidelines for a proper fit, but suggests that you investigate and understand your needs for the various items in the table below. The descriptions for each set up item follow below.

Bike Fit

Bike Set up	Specification	Your notes
Frame Geometry		
Saddle Height		
Saddle Angle		
Saddle fore/aft position		
Pedal/cleat position		
Stem height and length		
Handlebars		
Aerobar position and angle		

Frame geometry – The frame geometry is the measure of the angle of the seat tube with a road bike at 72 degrees and a tri bike at 75 degrees or steeper.

Saddle height – Your saddle can be raised or lowered depending on your leg length and the seat's fore/aft position relative to your bottom bracket or crank center. The goal with saddle height adjustment is to optimize a height that allows maximal power output from your legs while, at the same time, comfort for your crotch. Saddle height can change throughout the season for some athletes when they become stronger in the glut (butt) muscles and thus benefit from a change in saddle position.

This is a very important specification to set well, as even slight changes here can cause discomfort or injury, especially in your knees. Developing sore knees when riding is often a sign of the need to raise your seat.

According to some fit experts, your knee should have 25 to 30 degrees of flexion when the pedal is at the bottom-most point. Others set saddle height by measuring your inseam in centimeters and multiplying this measurement by 0.883. The top of the seat will be set at this distance from the center of the bottom bracket.

Most importantly, your hips should not rock back and forth when you pedal – if this happens then your saddle needs to be lowered.

Saddle angle – Since the angle of the saddle can change and affect your balance and comfort, this will be a personal choice. You will want to have your pelvis resting on a level surface, which may mean having the nose of the saddle a little higher than the rear. However, a saddle with the nose titled more down may be more comfortable. A level platform will allow you to find the best fore-aft position of the saddle and handlebar.

Saddle fore/aft – This position will depend on how you intend to use your bike. While the frame geometry (seat tube angle) plays a role in positioning the saddle relative to the cranks, the saddle positioning relative to the cranks, pedals and handlebars will make a difference in how you balance on your bike, hold an aerodynamic position and apply power both in and out of the saddle. In shorter distance triathlons, where comfort is not as much a concern, a more forward horizontal aerodynamic position with the seat will likely be desired. The saddle on a normal road or tour bike is behind the cranks so your body can be in balance, whereas the saddle on a track bike, where a lot of sprinting out of the saddle is done, will have a more forward saddle and handlebars to get more power over the cranks.

If you are new to cycling, go with what is comfortable first, then work toward a more forward aerodynamic position with the saddle.

Pedal/cleat position – The cleats on the bottom of your shoes clip into the pedals and can be slightly adjusted for unique body structures or predispositions to particular injuries. Cleats are positioned fore/aft so that the ball of your foot is directly over the axle of the pedal. Most newer road cleats allow greater degrees of rotational float to protect your knee. Cleat positions too far internally rotated may cause increased stress to the IT band.

Stem height and length – The stem of the handlebars needs to be in a position where you are able to place your hands on the handlebars with a comfortable reach. This will save your back, shoulders and neck from pain. Women with shorter torsos will often find this a key adjustment to make. Your elbows should have slight bend, and a light pressure on your hands. Comfort is the aim so you can ride in the drops or climb on the hoods without undue neck or back strain and perform optimally.

Handlebars – Handlebars come in a few different sizes, so if you are purchasing a stock generic bike, you may find it more comfortable to switch out the bars for a little narrower size. This is because women generally have shoulders narrower than men's. Some tri bikes come with tri bars – which are one piece bars with the aerobar and handlebar built together, such as Syntace bars.

Aerobar position and angle – Add on aerobars, such as Profile or Scott bars, which are a good aerodynamic aid. Ensure that the elbow pads are placed appropriately for a comfortable riding position.

Components

The component system of a bike is generally made by Shimano or Campangola. Each brand has several levels of quality and price. The main component set includes **shifters, derailleurs, brake levers and chain rings**.

Brake levers and pads – These are two of the most important parts of the bike you should ensure are working properly. Being able to stop on a dime and avoid serious accidents depend on good, functioning brake levers, cables and brake pads. Replace worn pads and make sure the brake cables are maintained with a little lube to ensure proper response to squeezing the brake levers.

Shifters – This is the part of the bike that allows you to change the gears of your front chain ring or your back cog set (also known as the cassette), so you are able to push the pace on the flats or spin quickly up a hard hill. Quality and well-maintained shifters are an essential part of a bike, just like a stick shift is for a car.

Wheels – The wheels of your bike are an important component because a poor quality bike wheel can result in loose or broken spokes, dented rims, or a seized hub. Such defects are hazardous to ride with so strong rims and spokes will not only save time and money in replacements and truing repairs, but also will improve your safety. Wheels also add a good amount of weight and wind resistance. Hence, finding a bike with lighter wheels, such as a Bontrager Race Lite or Zipp wheel, can save you time on the bike portion of your race if you wish to be more competitive.

Besides having an aerodynamic body position, wheels are the next item you can focus on to reduce your wind resistance on the bike. All those spokes cause a tremendous amount of turbulence that ends up slowing you down. That is why some people who are racing at faster speeds will choose to use solid disc wheels or trispoke wheels for serious aerodynamic improvements. Faster speeds increase the resistance, thus the use of better aerodynamic wheels is advantageous.

Other essential bike accessories

Helmet – This is an **absolute essential**. Do not be foolish enough to find yourself ever riding without one. Your life could depend on it. Most cyclists who have been riding for a while know of at least one situation where a helmet has saved them, or another rider, from serious injury.

In my one bike accident, my helmet cracked when I hit the pavement with my head but saved me from ending up six feet under. Most helmets meet ANSI safety standards. However, using a helmet more than 10 years old is not safe because the materials can break down. Make sure your helmet meets safety standards and that they demonstrate durability over many years, especially if you ride a lot in all-weather conditions. Consider that some of the more advanced streamline, lightweight helmets, which are comprised of very little material in an effort to keep them light, can potentially compromise their durability.

If you are doing longer training, or live in hotter environments, a light and well-ventilated helmet will be a must.

Before you leave the bike store, make sure you have fitted and adjusted the helmet straps for a snug, safe fit. You should not be able to push the helmet up over your forehead, nor should the helmet have a lot of side-to-side or front-to-back play. Most helmets come with padding that you can insert on the inside of the helmet to create a snug fit.

If you are a group ride leader or coach, never ever allow anyone to ride without a helmet, ever. The risk is not worth it. Even when riding in a parking lot, or practicing grass skills, the helmet should be worn. You never know when an unsuspecting car may rush out or if a fall will happen.

Spare tube and tire patch repair kit – Don't be caught without a spare tire or tools to repair a flat. Spares and patch kits can be kept in the back pocket of your cycling jersey or in a saddle bag that attaches under your saddle.

Essentials to carry with you include:

- Spare tubes (two is optimal as sometimes you can run through glass and puncture both tires)
- Patch kit
- Tire levers
- Spare Co_2 cartridges
- Allen keys or bike tool (for other repairs)
- ID and medical info
- Money
- Cell phone

Being unprepared without spare tubes or tools to change a flat is the fastest way to become unpopular with new riding partners or groups. The cardinal rule among cyclists is that you should always have the tools and tubes to be self-sufficient in the event of minor troubles such as a flat tire. This also means you should know HOW to change a flat.

Make sure you have the right size spare tube for your wheel size (either a 650 or 700c rim). Also, you may need to purchase tubes with long valve stems if you have wheels with deeper rims. Never assume your riding mates will have the correct tubes for your bike. Finally, for extra protection, there are tires you can purchase that have more puncture resistance (i.e., Kevlar tires).

Frame bike pump – This is a bike pump that fits on your frame, most often under the top tube. While a Co_2 cartridge can inflate tires, you never know how many flats or how much air you will need, and the bike pump on the frame is the most reliable way of ensuring your tires can be inflated. There are some compact double action frame pumps sold that do a great job if you put the pumping action in.

Floor bike pump – This is a stand up pump with a handle you can push down on and force air into the tire with more pressure than is usually possible with a frame pump. Frame pumps serve you well when you get a flat while on the road, but once home before your next ride, your tires are best inflated with a floor pump to full pressure (usually 120 PSI or higher). The tire will have the maximum recommended inflated pressure on the side of the tire wall. If you don't pump up your tires completely you can be susceptible to pinch flats or find it harder to ride due to more road resistance.

Road ID – You never know when emergencies or accidents will happen. If you require medical help, it is best to have your critical ID and medical info, including any allergies, with you on your bike or body with a wrist band, like Road ID. The Road ID is a convenient product to carry with you – either on your ankle, wrist or bike tube. It could safe your life if you are left unconscious after a serious accident.

Drinking system – Proper hydration is very important when you are riding, especially if you are in remote areas. Consider either water bottle cages to put on your bike or carry a Camelbak. Bottle cages can be added either on your down tube (two plugs are often already there) or, if you wish for something more aerodynamic or to bring additional supplies for longer riding, install one behind your saddle or in front with your aerobars. Front drink systems will also allow you to conveniently intake fluids without moving from the aerobar position.

Water bottles – There are many sizes and shapes of water bottles to choose from. The 16 oz and 24 oz bottles are most popular for cyclists. The most critical thing with your water bottles is ensuring that they fit in your cages snugly and won't fall out when riding over a bump. You may have to tighten your cages by bending the metal prongs that hold the bottles in place. Other bottle features include insulation, which is very beneficial in hotter climates. Adding ice to water bottles or freezing full bottles prior to hot summer rides are other ways to keep the contents cool and refreshing.

Lights or reflective materials – While riding at night or at dusk or dawn, a red blinking light is key for safety or visibility by other vehicles on the road. A light can be mounted on your seat post or on one of the back stays. Some saddle bags have clips for hooking lights on as well.

A front light will help you see where you are going. A front light can be headlamp on a headband or small light mounted on the handlebars.

More powerful halogen lights use larger rechargeable ni-cad batteries that sit in the water bottle cage, but there are quite a few less expensive, and lighter options with brightly flashing or strobe lights. For extra visibility, spoke lights can also be installed.

Cycling apparel – If comfort is your aim, padded bike shorts are essential. Note that many triathletes become accustomed to racing in swim or tri suits with little or no padding.

Bright, colorful jerseys will increase your visibility to motorists for additional safety. The best made jerseys will keep you comfortable in a variety of conditions and are made of materials, such as CoolMax or other breathable or sweat-wicking fibers. Most cycling jerseys, and even tri suits, also have back pockets that you can carry nutritional and personal items. With the growth of women in cycling and triathlon, many companies now offer more women-friendly designs and cuts. Check out women-friendly cycling gear at Sugoi and Terry Bicycles. Others, such as Zoot, JamSuits and Desoto, offer triathlon bottoms and tri suits with lighter padding so that you can wear the same clothing in the swim, bike and run, thus saving transition time.

An important aspect many beginners overlook is that wearing tight clothing with no flapping improves aerodynamics and reduces wind resistance. This could result in up to a 10% savings in energy expenditure.

Also, for more comfort and to prevent chaffing, don't make the mistake of wearing underwear under your shorts.

Bike chamois – This is the cushioning in your cycling shorts. It is available in many types of fabric. Generally, you will want more padding for longer rides. It is important to wash your shorts after each use to avoid yeast infections. If you are doing a multiday ride, hand wash your shorts each evening and hang dry or carry more than one pair of shorts. Many athletes get friction injuries (rubs, sores and blisters) after spending significant times on the saddle.

There are also special balms, such a Bike Balm, that you can apply to your chamois to reduce irritations.

Cold and wet weather attire – If you choose to ride in cold weather, you will need to gear yourself appropriately to make riding more pleasant and safe. For instance, it is dangerous to ride when you can't shift gears or brake successfully because you don't have warm gloves and your fingers are too cold to move.

Cold weather apparel includes:
- Moisture-wicking thermal underwear (such as Lifa or Underarmor)
- Arm warmers
- Leg warmers
- Plastic or rain repelling-jacket or vest
- Waterproof booties to cover cycling shoes (and keep feet and socks dry)
- Wool socks or other foot coverage that retain warmth and dry quickly
- Hat that fits under helmet
- Ski mask or balaclava (if very cold and you need to protect the skin on your face from freezing in the wind chill)
- Sunglasses or eye protection gear (since the winter sun can be even brighter and more damaging to your eyes due to the reflection of snow on the side of the road)
- Gloves (to keep your hands warm enough to function safely)

Rain apparel includes:
- Rain jacket that is water resistant but breathable (i.e., Goretex material with ventilation out the back or under the arms)
- Bright and reflective for better visibility in harsh conditions
- Lower back flap on jacket to keep rain off your butt
- Waterproof shoe covers or booties

Also, fenders attached to your bike will minimize the spray off your bike that may hit you or your fellow riders. This is an essential for group rides in wetter climates/cikes, like Seattle.

Cycling gloves Many cyclists are accustomed to wearing cycling gloves. However, this is less prominent for triathletes. The padding in the palm of the gloves, usually some kind of gel, offers protection from the vibrations that come from the road through the handlebars and to the hands. Triathlon racers rarely wear cycling gloves during competition since changing during transitions is too cumbersome and time consuming.

In the winter, it is essential to find full coverage gloves that allow for your hands to keep warm enough to be able to firmly grip the handlebars, brakes and shifters.

Cycling socks – There is a wide assortment of lightweight and fashionable ankle-height socks for cycling. Brands such as DeFeet and Sock Guy offer diverse selections of designs that inspire or add humor to a cyclist's feet. In wet conditions, waterproof brands, such as Sealskinz, help ensure drier feet conditions for riders.

During races, some triathletes do not wear socks in order to reduce the transition time.

RUN

Running is a sport that seems simple to equip for because the basics are just running shoes and comfortable attire. However, outfitting yourself with the proper shoes, given the ample market choices, can be a challenging task.

Thorough analysis of your feet and running biomechanics, along with your training needs, should be considered when making your shoe purchases. Do not skimp on shoes to save a few bucks because having high quality, properly fitting shoes will save you from injuries and pains caused by running in poor footwear.

Seek help at a running specialty store staffed with knowledgeable employees. Tell them about your situation, any previous injuries or pains, and your past shoe experiences. Have them look at the wear pattern on your last pair of runners, or even better, have them watch you run to help them consider the kind of support features best for you. The salesperson should ask you about your running goals – how often, how long, and whether you run on track, roads, or trails.

Try many models – everyone has different feet. Find the model that offers the right fit for you with respect to width, support for pronation (straight or curve lasted), cushioning, weight (training or race flat), and tread (trail or road). The shoes should feel very comfortable in the store. Anything that feels like it rubs a little now will feel even worse when you hit the road. There is no such thing as breaking in a running shoe with regard to comfort.

Shoe manufactures have improved their designs for women, making models specifically for women and truly designed for a woman's foot and biomechanical needs.

As you develop your strength and running form, the type of shoe best for you can often change. Motion control and cushioning are best for beginners new to running. Proper fit is key for more advanced runners who are pounding the streets many miles.

Night running apparel – Your Safety is a key concern when running at night. Reflective strips on running shoes, running tights or jackets helps improve your visibility to motorists, as well as a bright flashing light strapped on your arm or a bright reflective vest.

Sport bras – Running enjoyment is enhanced significantly for women when they have proper support to prevent excessive motion of the breasts, as well as a bra design that does not cause chafing to the nipple or other areas of the breast. Also, finding a design and material that doesn't dig into the shoulders or skin around the chest is important. For extra support while running in a triathlon, women will often wear a sport bra under the swim suit. Two sport bras are sometimes even necessary for large-breasted women.

Look to such brands as Sugoi, Champion, and Terry for women friendly fits.

Running shorts, tights and tops – The best options for clothing while running are those items made of materials that wick sweat and are seamless so they prevent chafing.

Lycra and CoolMax are popular materials. Shorts often have liners so that you don't need separate underwear. Avoid cotton materials since cotton easily gets wet and cold and can chafe your skin.

Run socks – Socks should be blister-free, dry, cool, and not cotton! Some socks have extra padding to make your feet more comfortable when pounding on the pavement. However, make sure these thicker socks still fit in your shoes. As in cycling, there are several brands that offer colorful and cute designs.

Many women choose not to wear socks in short triathlons to save time on transitions, but it is suggested you rehearse this to see if you are blister prone without socks, especially when your feet are wet after pouring water over your body at aid stations to keep cool in hot climes. The swim portion also "softens" your feet, so they are more blister prone.

Protection from the sun is necessary due to the duration of triathlon events and the fact that many take place in sunny areas surrounded by water. It is critical to protect your skin and eyes from the damage the sun can do. Proper eyewear, skin coverage and waterproof sunscreen lotions will help minimize your risk to premature wrinkling and serious skin cancer. If you are training or racing outside all day, especially if you are swimming or sweating a lot, make sure that you re-apply your sunscreen periodically.

Consider **a hat, sunglasses and sunscreen as triathlon essentials,** no less important than your helmet, to keep your skin and eyes protected from the damaging rays of the sun.

Add ons for the serious tri woman: Advanced training and racing equipment

When considering whether or not to spend more money on equipment or triathlon products, keep in mind that triathlon is meant to be a healthy hobby that enhances your life. Don't feel pressure to spend more than you can afford or put yourself under financial pressure just to keep up with the excess consumerism in sport.

There are frugal options to purchasing some of the more advanced and pricey tri gear, such as used items on Ebay auctions or other web site classifieds.

It is interesting to note the findings of a 2000 survey of 925 multisport athletes by USA Triathlon:

- 35% value their bike at $2,000-$4,000; 18% spend $1,500-$2,000.
- Most triathletes (28%) spend $50-$100 on swim equipment; 23% spend $25-$50 on swim equipment.
- 36% spend less than $300 on their bike equipment; 22% spend $1,000-$3000 on their bike equipment; 19% spend $300-$500.
- 54% spend $100-$299 on their running equipment; 26% spend $300-$500.

(USAT Demographic report, 2005)

Below are some of the tri gear options you may consider if you are more advanced and committed to the sport.

SWIM

Triathlon wet suit – This becomes an essential in colder water temperatures or longer swimming races, especially for leaner women. Triathlon wet suits are allowed when the temperatures are in the 70s (or approximately 20 degrees Celsius). However, if the water temperature is too warm (78 degrees or higher at USAT races), race officials will announce it as a non wet suit swim. Some U.S. races will allow you to race with a wetsuit even if it is declared a non-wet suit swim, but swimmers with wet suits are ineligible for awards and rankings.

Triathlon wet suits come in sleeveless or full sleeves, which will offer more protection from colder water. The main difference from normal scuba wet suits is that triathlon wet suits are designed for free movement in the shoulders and the thickness of the rubber varies in different areas of the suit.

The fitting of a wetsuit is the most important factor in order to prevent water coming into the suit, chafing or restricted motion (particularly for full-sleeve suits). Ironman wet suits has a FemmeForm suit particularly designed for women.

Shellie Oroshiba in her wetsuit in the transition area, ready to race

Wet suits can help with buoyancy, as well, and improve swim times for those who are less advanced swimmers.

Swim Aids

Pull buoy – This is a floating aid that goes between your knees or lower legs to allow your legs to float behind you while you use just your upper body to swim. Isolating the upper body provides more resistance to work more on upper body strength and coordination without the use of your legs to kick. Most pools will have these as part of the equipment, but it is nice to have a pull bouy of your own.

Pull buoys are also useful for triathletes because they can somewhat mimic the buoyancy of a wet suit. Some people find they swim faster with a pull buoy, which is a good indicator that there is a balance issue still to be corrected. This will be discussed further in the swim skills section.

Fins or flippers – These are used to help focus on developing a more effective kick by recruiting more leg muscles and demanding more ankle flexibility. Flippers can also help elevate the heart rate or intensity if it is desired to make the workout harder. Fins will also enhance ankle flexibility, an important part of an effective kick. Fins will allow you to pick up your speed and "feel" fast, swimming better as well. There are short fins and longer fins; the longer the fins, the more resistance they provide.

Kickboards – Generally, these floating boards are used to focus on your kick and strengthen your legs since your arms hold onto the board and your legs do the work. Kicking drills can also be done without a kickboard (as will be introduced in the swim skills section). For a different twist, a kickboard can also be put between the legs like a pull buoy and help with core rotation.

Paddles – Paddles are a swim tool worn on your hands. They are usually made of flat plastic of varying shapes and sizes, depending on how much resistance you wish to impose on your upper body. They help isolate the upper body and will cause more resistance against the water, thus making the arm muscles apply more force during the stroke and help build strength. However, some swimmers put too much strain on their shoulders by using paddles and cause injury. Paddles will also help you to move more effectively through the water and develop stronger elbow and hand positions.

BIKE

These additions to the bike can be considered non-essential for safety, but can lead to more effective training and performances. Consider adding this bike equipment or gear (listed here in order of importance) to improve your cycling power, comfort and aerodynamics.

1. Clipless pedals and cycling shoes with cleats

This would be the first priority for an accessory addition once you have basics. Having pedals that clip to your cycling shoes (via cleats on the bottom of your shoes) will allow you full use of your leg power for the complete pedal stroke. This will be most noticeable when cycling uphill where you will be able pull up with your shoe, as well as push down. They are called clipless because they have no toe cages or toe clips, which can make riding dangerous.

A variety of systems are available and are a matter of personal preference. Look, Speedplay, Time and SPD are some of the major brands offering clipless pedals.

2. Aero bike items

In addition to aerobars, other aero features can be added to your bike to make your bike more streamlined. Aero wheels with deep rims, and/or flat bladed spokes or a tri spoke will have less wind resistance than a wheel with plenty of round spokes. Other parts can be made more aero friendly, such as seat posts, drinking systems or brake levers. This will make more of a difference when you are traveling at faster speeds closer to 40 kilometers per hour.

3. Cycling computer
(cyclometer or heart rate monitor with cycling functions)

There are a large range of odometers or cycling computers out there that are just cyclometers measuring speed, distance, and giving time of day. They measure with a transmitter fixed to a wheel. Others are more complex and may provide altitude, cadence and heart rate information, as well.

Cat Eye, Specialized, and Polar are a few of the major brands to investigate if you feel you will benefit from more data feedback on your cycling performance.

4. Wind trainer or rollers

When you need to train indoors through the winter or during inclement weather conditions, a wind trainer or rollers are the best options. A wind trainer places the front wheel on a block and the rear wheel of your bike on a resistant wheel that spins around as you ride in place. The resistance can be adjusted to your needs. These trainers are often loud, so if you live on the second floor of an apartment, your neighbors below might not enjoy your workouts as much as you do.

There are many different trainers on the market, with CompuTrainer or Trax providing the most data and programmable capabilities. You can set a particular course to ride or set yourself against opponents while watching the computer monitor.

5. Power meter

Being able to measuring your power output while riding can be a powerful tool for feedback. The power readings will give an objective perspective of the intensity of the workout relative to test standards. SRM or Power-Tap are the best-known power meters used. The SRM is the most expensive of the power meters, costing upward of $3,000 a unit. But for some professionals, the data and immediate feedback provided is critical to their performance so the cost is worth it. Most amateurs will opt for the Power-Tap models that retail for less than $1,000, however they tend not to be as functional nor durable.

RUN

Inserts for additional support – These support items might be more of an essential to the beginner who is injured or with a biomechanical imbalance that can be corrected with orthopedics or arch supports. Heel cups will also help runners prone to plantar fasciitis.

Lace locks or elastic laces – These are a must for those who hope to have speedy transitions. If you can avoid tying your shoe laces in transition, you will save time. Lace locks or elastic laces allow you to slip into you shoes without challenging your knot-tying skills.

OTHER

Heart rate monitor (HRM) – A wide range of HRMs are available in many places, from sports stores to fitness clubs to direct online purchases from the dealer. HRMs are a useful tool for determining your intensity while you train and can direct you, like a coach on your wrist, with beeps to indicate wether you are in the desired zone, as determined in the target settings you have pre-selected. HRMs help you to be more effective with your training, keeping the hard days hard, the easy days easy and help reveal times when you may be working too hard and need to scale back.

Sally Edward's book *The Heart Rate Monitor Guidebook to Heart Zone Training* is one resource that explains the heart rate zones in relation to your fitness program.

Assessment tools – As you become more advanced, a more detailed analysis of your swim stroke is beneficial. Thus, tools like an underwater swim camera for underwater video may be desirable. Many swim coaches in your area will often already have such tools and you can book a private lesson with them to be videotaped and then review your stroke on camera with you.

Finding woman-friendly products and services in triathlon

There are many places where you can find products for the multisport woman. Web site shopping is a fast and easy way to make effective purchases. There are a few online sites dedicated to women's sports gear and/or triathlon specifically.

Web sites for Triathlon Gear

Women Only

www.title9sports.com	*women's athletic clothing*
www.danskin.com	*women's triathlon and athletic clothing*
www.teamestrogen.com	*women's tri apparel and wet suits*
www.trichics.com	
www.terrybicycles.com	

Triathlon Gear and Clothing
www.totaltri.com
www.trisports.com
www.tri-zone.com
www.trigeeks.ca

Swim Gear and Clothing
www.keifer.com
www.swim2000.com
http://www.swim-city.com

Cycling Gear and Clothing
www.performancebike.com
www.nashbar.com

Running Shoes and Clothing
www.roadrunnersports.com

Bargain Sites

www.swimoutlet.com	*discount swim gear, triathlon clothing and wet suits*
www.sportsbasement.com	*discount and closeout clothing and gear*

PART 2

Get Moving

CHAPTER 4

Basic Training Principles

This chapter will serve as an introduction to the basic fitness training principles useful for triathlon training. To keep things simple and avoid a complex discussion on physiology and biochemistry, we will limit the discussion to three principles key to triathlon training: aerobic endurance training, anaerobic training, and lactate threshold. These principles are similar for men and women and are applied to training through categorizing different intensity zones and heart rate measurements. Additional aspects of fitness include strength and flexibility.

It is also important to understand that fitness improvements occur when a balanced mix of training, such as aerobic exercise, strength training and stretching sessions, also incorporate recovery aspects. Growth occurs only if you allow the body to recover and adapt following training stress.

Whether you are new to triathlon or a veteran of the sport, these are the fundamentals to guide your fitness development.

BASIC TRAINING PHYSIOLOGY

Aerobic training – If there is one thing to remember about basic physiology for triathlon training, it is that aerobic development and endurance is vital. With the exception of very short distance triathlons, any triathlon event will primarily demand use of your aerobic system. Aerobic means using oxygen, or O_2, for energy production for movement in swimming, biking and running.

Developing aerobic endurance is the foundation to success in triathlon. Just as a house or tall building requires a solid foundation to build upon, a focus on establishing your aerobic foundation will support more stress, and hence the capability to sustain a higher level of intensity in training and racing. It takes many years to develop endurance capacity to compete at a high level.

The adaptations your body make as a result of using oxygen for training efforts include more capillary development to assist in delivering oxygen via blood to muscles and more cellular machinery to assist in oxygen metabolism. These developments make your body more aerobically efficient, but only occur with lower training intensities when oxygen is available and used.

Anaerobic training and lactate threshold – As you increase your intensity of exercise by swimming, biking or running faster, you will reach a level where oxygen metabolism is no longer possible and your body converts to anaerobic (without oxygen) metabolism. Anaerobic training results in a by-product called lactate, or lactic acid, which literally poisons the muscle cells with its high acidity. Lactate threshold is the line under which you can sustain a certain intensity while still flushing out the debilitating lactate to keep it below harmful levels. If you go over the threshold you will soon have to slow down or stop as a result of your muscles no longer being able to function. A fit female can run a 10-kilometer race at her threshold and a mile above threshold with good anaerobic endurance.

INTENSITY ZONES AND HEART RATE

Heart Rate (HR) – The rate at which your heart beats is a reflection of how hard you are making your cardiovascular system work. An increase in heart rate can be a result of exercise, stress, or an alarming situation. It is important to note that the heart rate at certain exercise intensities is not always comparable between individuals. Heart rate guidelines are best developed for each individual by incorporating one's unique fitness level, exercise history, training goals and sport-specific focus.

There are various ways to measure your heart rate. Wrist or neck pulse checks have often been used to get a rough estimate. However, the best measurement tool is a heart rate monitor. The technology of a heart rate monitor (a watch and a transmitter chest strap) allows you to make more precise training decisions and thus reach your goals more efficiently.

Maximum HR – The highest number of heartbeats in a minute that your heart is capable of reaching during maximal effort is your max HR. This level is different for everyone as it is genetically determined and not consistently age-dependent as past exercise programs may have assumed.

There are a number of ways to test your maximum HR, including a max stress test by a physician or sports physiologist, running a 5k race with full out sprint to the finish, or biking to the top of a long hill as fast as you can and recording the top HR reached. Other, more sophisticated testing can be done in a lab and can include lactate testing or MVO_2 (maximum volume of oxygen) testing. These are more effective testing options to use in determining your training heart rate zones. Some fitness centers or universities offer this kind of testing.

If you are returning to exercise and/or you are not very fit, a maximal test is not wise since the stress can potentially cause harm, such as injury to muscles or tendons not yet strong enough to sustain the strain of a max effort. Sub-maximal efforts, such as running an aerobic mile test where you stay consistently at your estimated aerobic baseline heart rate (described on the following page) can also help estimate HR zones or your pacing in each zone.

Remember also that you will have a specific max and range of intensities for each sport. Greater muscle recruitment in running, as well as it being a weight-bearing sport, means that the max HR for running will typically be higher than for biking and swimming. This might also depend on your mastery level of each sport. A highly experienced cyclist can often reach higher HRs on the bike than she does on the run.

HEART RATE TRAINING ZONES

The typical calculation for maximum HR in the fitness industry for women has been 226 – your age. This is an outdated method and not valid for the majority of people.

Once you have completed a max test or sub-max assessment, you can establish your heart rate zones for the kind of training you intend to do. The best known categories have been developed by coaching guru Joel Friel, author of *The Triathlete's Training Bible*, and Sally Edwards, author of *The Heart Rate Monitor Guidebook to Heart Zone Training*.

Five Heart Rate Zones
Zone 1 – 50-60% Max HR – Low intensity or recovery zone; this zone burns fat for fuel
Zone 2 – 60-75% Max HR – Aerobic training zone; this zone burns more fat than carbohydrates for fuel
Zone 3 – 75-85% Max HR – Intensive aerobic zone; increase in carbohydrate that is burned
Zone 4 – 80-90% Max HR – Threshold zone; this is the line where unmanageable lactate levels result in exercise being done in the absence of oxygen or anaerobic. Well conditioned athletes can sustain this level for approximately an hour.
Zone 5 – 90-100% Max HR – Anaerobic zone; this zone can be sustained for only a few minutes at a time due to lactate production. This zone burns carbohydrates.

Aerobic baseline – As mentioned above, triathlon training involves mainly aerobic endurance training. Phil Maffetone devised an easy way to estimate your aerobic baseline heart rate, which you should stay under in order to stay in the most beneficial aerobic endurance training zone. He called it Maximum Aerobic Heart Rate (MAHR).

Calculate your MAH by following the steps below.
1. 180 – age
2. Add or subtract based on category of athlete
   a. never trained before, serious illness operation – subtract 10
   b. currently exercise inconsistently, injury, colds in past year – subtract 5
   c. past year worked out consistently, progressed fitness – subtract 0
   d. compete, improved performance over past 2 years, no more than 2 colds – add 5

Your aerobic max using the Maffetone method:
1. 180 – _____ (your age) = _____ (+/- category of fitness above) = _____ MAH

If you do an aerobic mile running test where you hold consistent at your MAH plus or minus 2 beats while running three to five miles on a track and collect your mile split times, you can estimate your other zones and pacing in those zones.

For instance, a MAH at 158 and a 9:30 to 10:00 min mile pace would have estimated zones and paces at the following rates:

Zone	Mile Pace	Heart Rate
Zone 5	below 8	185+
Zone 4	8:00-8:30	175-185
Zone 3	8:30-9:30	158-170
Zone 2	9:30-10:00	150-158
Zone 1	10:00+	‹ 150

Perceived effort scale

If you do not have a heart rate monitor, you can still subjectively assess your intensity. This is not always the most effective method since various factors, such as heat, hydration, fatigue, and altitude can change your heart rates. The PE scale is from 1-20 with 1 being very, very easy and 20 being very, very hard. Aerobic training benefits come from staying around the 10-14 PE levels.

Strength – After aerobic endurance, strength is the next most important component of fitness. Once you have built your endurance with aerobic training, you will want to increase your strength in order to sustain a higher force output. This will lead to a stronger swim stroke, pedal stroke or running stride, particularly on hilly terrain. Strength training is something that most women can reap huge benefits from.

Many women shy away from strength training because they don't like male-dominated gyms, feel uncertain about what exercises to do and how to do them, or they have a fear of bulking up. Unless you are hitting the gym for several hours daily, or have the genetic make-up to become a body builder, there should be little concern that you will bulk up. Many fitness facilities are now a lot more proactive about making women feel welcome and comfortable with attention to cleanliness, women-friendly weights and equipment, and staff to assist. It is strongly recommended that you consult with a certified strength trainer to have an assessment done and receive instruction on how to use various equipment. Additionally, a certified strength trainer can check your form. Proper form is critical to getting the most out of strength training, especially for injury prevention as you increase resistance or the amount of weight you are lifting.

The best kind of strength training exercises for triathlon are dynamic strength exercises, which use multiple muscle groups through a range of motion, and core stability exercises. There are plenty of beneficial exercises you can do, whether with weights, balls, or tubing in the gym or with force applications in sport-specific situations, such as big gear cycling or swimming with paddles.

Consult a book like *Strength Training for Women* by Lori Incledon, *Strength Ball Training* by Lorne Goldenberg and Peter Twist, or the *Ultimate Core Ball Workout* by Jeanine Detz.

Reasons for strength training
- Gain stamina for longer and harder triathlon training
- Enhance efficiency with greater core stability

- Prevent injury by gaining greater stability and muscular support while in motion
- Build more muscle with positive effects on metabolism
- Build stronger, denser bones to help prevent osteoporosis

Flexibility – Developing and maintaining your flexibility is a key component for triathlon training. The demands of all three sports require a good range of motion and fluid form for greater efficiency, which is critical for longer distance training and racing. Chronically tight muscles or joints can decrease the range and power of your swim stroke or running stride, for instance, and worse, can cause poor form or compensations that lead to injury.

Many triathletes don't take the time to stretch or participate in a yoga class until they are injured or excessively tight and experience pain when swimming, cycling or running. Chronic injuries can be prevented through proper attention to flexibility.

It is beneficial to be proactive with flexibility exercises, such as dynamic stretching or yoga. Finish each training session, particularly higher intensity sessions, with a cool down involving slower motion exercise and specific stretches or a yoga routine that covers the important muscles and joints used most in training. Think of it as your first opportunity to recover and rejuvenate yourself.

Consider developing your own routine from head to toe, or vice versa, to cover the main body parts you need to give attention to. Because I had a serious neck injury after a bike accident many years ago, I started with my neck, then moved to my shoulders and arms, then my back and quad, hamstring and glut muscles. I would finish with ankle stability exercises. More recently, I have incorporated regular yoga, either in a class or following a video or DVD like Rodi Yee's *Yoga for Athletes* or Caron Shepley's *Yoga for Endurance Athletes*. To consider the range of stretches beneficial for each sport, consult a detailed book like Bob Anderson's *Stretching*.

Recovery – Recovery is an essential component of training. Recovery enables you to improve your fitness and become stronger and faster.

Many driven women do not give this key aspect of training enough attention in their training plans. As a result, they do not reap the full rewards of an aerobic endurance and strength conditioning program.

Recovery can be total rest or non-activity, or light, rejuvenating exercise that facilitates the repair of fatigued muscles and refreshes your mental state. Restorative yoga or light swimming can be among the best options to aid in recovery.

Poor recovery will compromise subsequent training sessions. A few signs of poor recovery are higher heart rate when waking, insomnia, poor appetite or sugar cravings, irritability or depressed mood.

Women who live busy lives and are already overstretched with work, family and community activities will find it more difficult to recover from intense training sessions. Your lifestyle stress will have a major impact on your ability to recover more rapidly from training stress. Many women today are subjected to what author Brent Bost calls the "hurried woman syndrome" in his book by the same title. He offers practical strategies to balancing the stressful life of many multitasking women in today's society. More will be discussed on this topic in Chapter 12.

WOMEN'S ISSUES IN TRAINING AND PERFORMANCE

Over time, women have shown their resilience to training and enduring in the sport of triathlon as men do. As the doors have opened for women to participate in more and more sporting events, women have proven that a high level of athletic success is possible despite their differences from men. As more women engage in sport and achieve feats once thought unhealthy for women, more research has documented gender similarities and differences. In fact, in ultra endurance running events, some women have proven to have better endurance than the men. Perhaps a woman's genetic make up that supports child bearing, and the greater body fat percentages compared to men, make women more suitable for ultra endurance events. There is also anecdotal evidence of many female swimmers having a greater recovery capacity than men following high-intensity training. This may be due to slightly different hormones, body composition, and the effect of those factors on recovery.

Hormone levels in women's bodies can create differences in physiology and present challenges in peaking for events physically and mentally during different times of the monthly cycle. Pre-menstrual syndrome symptoms, such as bloating and moodiness, can certainly make competing in a triathlon an extra challenge. It is interesting to note, however, that studies on the impact of menstruation and hormone changes on athletic performance are somewhat inconclusive. So it many not be as much of a disadvantage for women as some would like to think. Furthermore, hormones and childbirthing experience may be a reason women seem to have higher pain thresholds and endurance.

The structure of women's bodies with wider hips and a tendency for "knock knees" can result in a greater prevalence of biomechanical issues for knees, feet and hips while running and cycling. As well, breasts can cause various challenges physically and mentally for women participating in a sport as body conscious as triathlon. Thankfully, advances in sport bra fit and function now provide the opportunity for many more large breasted women to enjoy running.

On a mental level, women tend to have different issues than men when it comes to balancing child care and career, emotional well-being and competition, social bonding and self time.

Menstrual cycle and training and performance for female athletes

A number of studies have been done on the menstrual cycle and its impact on performance and physiology. The following presents a basic outline of the menstrual cycle phases, hormone levels and presents results of those investigations on the impact on training and performance.

Table 7
Phases of menstrual cycle

Phase	Duration	Hormone levels
Follicular phase	Lasts average of 14 days, but can vary from 7-21 days.	Estrogen levels begin very low and rise during this phase.
Ovulation	When an egg is released. In some cycles an egg may not be released. This is called anovulatory.	Estrogen levels reach a maximum just prior to ovulation and then level off. Lutenizing hormone, released by the anterior pituitary gland, peaks.
Luteal phase	Occurs after ovulation and on average lasts 12-14 days.	Progesterone levels peak in the middle of this phase then decline. Body temperature also rises.
Menstrua-tion	Begins with the onset of menstrual bleeding.	

(Source: Bernhardt, G. [1999] The Female Cyclist. Gearing up a level. Boulder, Colorado: Velopress)

Estrogen and progesterone factors

(from Lebrun, C. and Rumball, J. [2001] "Relationship Between Athletic Performance and Menstrual Cycle". *Current Women's Health Reports*, 1, 232-240.)

- Estrogen increases lipid synthesis. Female athletes use more fat for energy than males. This is offered as a contributing factor for a women's greater capacity for ultra endurance events.
- Estrogen protects bone density.
- Some limited studies have shown reduced aerobic capacity associated with high estrogen levels.
- Estrogen levels are the highest at the end of the follicular phase.
- Progesterone is highest during the luteal phase.
- Progesterone is the hormone responsible for increased body temperature (.3-.5° Celsius) during the luteal phase.

Menstrual cycle studies on training and performance for female athletes
A number of studies have found some interesting, yet inconclusive results, regarding the impact of a woman's menstrual cycle on various aspects of female athletic performance. When considering the changes in hormones, body temperature, and body weight during different phases, researchers have looked at the impact on anaerobic endurance, strength and injury susceptibility for female athletes.

An article published in *Current Women's Health Reports* by C. Lebrun, and J. Rumball titled "Relationship Between Athletic Performance and Menstrual Cycle" found that women who exercise at the same intensity level have a higher heart rate during the luteal phase. This might mean that female athletes are disadvantaged in high heat and humidity when they train and compete during the luteal phase due to an already increased body temperature and heart rate. After a review of many studies, the authors wrote that there is not conclusive evidence of significant difference in athletic performance at any phase in the menstrual cycle. This, however, does not mean that there are no differences. Lebrun further cited that most studies to date have been highly limited and that atypical menstrual cycles in many female athletes further complicates the ability of researchers to study this effectively.

An interesting study by G. Masterson looked at the impact of menstrual phases on anaerobic power performance and found that among active collegiate women, those in the luteal phase had better peak power and were less fatigued at the completion of their exercise than women in the follicular phase.

Further study on the effect of the different phases of the menstrual cycle and oral contraceptives on athletic performance concluded that 37-67% of female athletes polled reported no detriment in athletic performance during menstruation, while 13-39% reported improvements in performance.

However, studies more recently concluded there is no significant variation in muscle strength or endurance between women in early follicular, ovulation and mid-luteal phases of menstrual cycle (Friden, et al., 2003). Another study found that neither maximal or sub-maximal exercise performance is affected by the menstrual cycle phase, at sea level or at high altitudes (Beidleman, et al., 1999).

An interesting discovery documented in the journal of *American Orthopedic Society for Sports Medicine* in 1998 found an association between the menstrual cycle and anterior cruciate ligament injuries. Female athletes have anterior cruciate ligament (knee) injury eight times more than men. A 2002 report in the *Journal of Athletic Training* saw greater incidence of ACL injuries on days 1 or 2 of women's menstrual cycles. However, a 2004 study published in *American Orthopedic Society for Sports Medicine* reported that knee laxity does not vary with the menstrual cycle, before or after exercise, thus suggesting that knee laxity is not a plausible explanation for greater ACL injury.

Managing monthly success for the tri woman

For all females, it is important to recognize how you experience the monthly cycle of hormones, pre-menstrual symptoms (PMS), cramps during menstruation, or other effects of nature's "gift."

Every woman experiences a myriad of symptoms and effects unique to her. In fact, more than 150 PMS symptoms have been identified. Over the years, I've begun to recognize my pre-menstrual plight to include:

- Bloating
- Sore breasts
- Extreme difficulty waking in the mornings due to feeling "drugged," which is different from normal exhaustion or fatigue
- Emotional sensitivity and tearfulness
- Aggression and easily angered
- Decrease in hand dexterity and increase in dropping things
- Fat and sugar cravings

I've also recognized that during this pre-menstrual time frame, I've had some of my best athletic performances notably in the sport of rowing, which demands more power and anaerobic output than triathlon. This concurs with the study noted above by Masterson, where it was found that those in the luteal phase had better peak power and were less fatigued at the completion of their exercise than women in the follicular phase.

Women have been competing for years at every stage of the menstrual cycle with little documented limitations. My experience with competing during every stage of the menstrual cycle is that, with the exception of the first day of my period where I'm non-functional due to debilitating cramps, there is little physical difference and that the cursed feelings of PMS have little meaning to my performances. At the very least, this allows me to approach training and racing with more peace and self-understanding.

I encourage you to track your menstrual cycle and PMS symptoms over a number of years and consider the relationship with your training and life stress, your body composition (especially if you are very lean), and the quality of your nutrition.

- Consider logging your changes in heart rate or perceived effort during PMS and menstruation. Extra fatigue may indicate a need to assess iron levels.
- Examine your nutrition during the normal part of your cycle and the pre-menstrual phase and consider how your PMS or menstrual cramps are affected by the intake of caffeine, refined sugar, high fiber fruits and vegetables or other nutritional particulars.

Other helpful tips include:

- Supplementation with magnesium and calcium is reported to help many who suffer from PMS.
- Consider manipulating your cycle with a contraceptive pill that eliminates the fluctuations in hormones that cause PMS.
- Schedule your recovery off weeks at the same time as your PMS phase to be gentler to your body when it already feels in turmoil.

The Female Athletic Triad

Because many female endurance athletes under-eat, they thus lack nourishment with essential nutrients, and at the same time put tremendous strain on the body with intense training regimens, there is often a combination of eating disorders, amenorrhea and stress fractures. This is known as the Female Athletic Triad.

Oligoamenorrhea (irregular menstruation) and amenorrhea (absence of menses entirely) are common among female endurance athletes. Without menses (via menopause or the above), hormonal levels change dramatically. A detrimental result of a lack of estrogen is the loss of bone density, thus increasing the risk of stress fractures.

An important point to consider in this female affliction is that many professionals point to lack of body fat or lean body composition below the 10 percent fat considered "healthy" for women as the reason for irregular or absent menses. The reality is that many very lean triathletes still experience regular menstrual cycles, while some in the healthy body fat zone may not. The key difference I've observed, with both myself and other women, is quality nutrition adequate to support the stress demands of the athlete's training regimen and lifestyle.

Because of the weight-bearing nature of triathlon, coupled with the body-conscious attire of swimsuits and tight lycra race suits, women face significant challenges in staying healthy through a diet that supports training demands and body repair needs. More on nourishment for the female body will follow in Chapter 10.

CHAPTER 5
Sport Skills in Swim, Bike, Run

CREATING FOUNDATIONS

Regardless of your level as an athlete, technique is key for creating strong foundations, better efficiency and preventing injury. This chapter will discuss some of the best skill foundations and drills you can consider incorporating into your training sessions.

While many will skip drill practices, it is important for women to learn efficient form that will allow you to swim, bike and run longer, with less effort, energy consumption, or biomechanical issues that may cause injuries later. Adding a focus to your movement will provide you with more longevity and fun later. Whether your aim is to be fit and healthy for the rest of your life, or to compete at higher levels in the triathlon world, creating a solid foundation of good form through repeated and perfected drill practice will be doing your body a favor.

SWIM LIKE A MERMAID

Good swimming form is particularly important for women since it helps address anxiety issues they often experience in the water. Efficient, smooth form results in better ability to breathe, relax and be comfortable in the water. The Total Immersion method is popular in the U.S. with clinics around the country to help swimmers approach swimming with a systematic method. Check out www.totalimmersion.net for useful videos and books to turn non-swimmers into streamlined, fluid mermaids in the water.

Two swim principles: Minimize drag and maximize propulsion

There are only two things you need to remember in order to swim effectively:
1. Minimize your drag so that you are a streamlined vessel that slips easily through the water.
2. Maximize your propulsion so that you effectively use your body to glide through the water.

If in doubt, think like a streamlined torpedo ripping through the water, or a graceful mermaid flowing effortlessly.

Three ways to minimize drag:
1. Balance your body so that your legs are not dragging behind and slowing you down.
2. Streamline your body like a light, tight torpedo rather than being like a floppy fish.
3. Swim more on your side rather than like a flat tub.

Three ways to maximize propulsion:
1. Work the stroke its full range of motion, through the shoulders to hips utilizing the core.

2. Increase power through synchronization or flow, not sheer muscle effort.
3. Become sensitive to using your hands as paddles moving water.

Identify two areas listed above that you can improve upon and then look for three to five drills you can utilize to refine your awareness and effectiveness of movement in the water. Because swimming is such a highly coordinated skill, practicing these drills with smooth deliberate action each time you are in the water will be helpful. It takes plenty of practice, so be patient.

If you are not practicing with a triathlon or masters swim club already, you should try to get someone like a masters swim coach (check out www.usms.org for chapters and clubs in the U.S.) to video tape you and review areas you can improve. If you are new to swimming and not ready for a group program, there are also a number of clinics around the country for women only (see Chapter 7) that can assist you in a non-intimidating environment.

Darlene Hall and her friend at the World Ironman Championships ready to swim and have fun.

Below is a list of drills that I have used for my women-only swim group for five years now. These drills have helped turn hundreds of women into streamlined, balanced mermaids.

Drill name	Purpose	Description
Streamlines	Balance, streamline	Pushing off the wall in tight torpedo like position
Streamline kicking hand lead	Balance, streamline	Kicking on stomach with hands leading in tight torpedo-like balanced position
Streamline kicking head lead	Balance, streamline	Kicking on stomach with hands at sides, holding balanced, streamlined position

Drill name	Purpose	Description
Streamline hand lead rolling side to side	Balance, streamline and swim on side	Kicking on stomach with hands in front, then roll entire body to one side, then over to the other side. Breathe when on your stomach and repeat.
Streamline head lead roll	Balance, streamline and swim on side	Kicking on stomach with hands at side in streamline, then roll entire body to one side, then through to the other side. When back on stomach, breathe and repeat.
Side kicking left or right with hand leading	Balance on side, swim on side	Push off the wall while straight on your stomach with hands leading, then roll completely to the side with one arm leading and the other arm on the thigh. Find your balance on your side – pressing shoulder and head down. Rest head on the outstretched arm. Arm and hand should be in the "ready" position – palm down and elbow rolled up and arm stretched out straight in line with YOUR body.
Side kick 6-6	Balance, streamline and swim on side, head position, arm propulsion	Push off the wall while straight on your stomach with hands leading, then roll completely to the side with one arm leading and other arm on thigh. Find balance on your side– pressing shoulder and head down resting on arm. Then take one stroke, initiating with the front arm – keep a high elbow and put hand into the water with fingers facing down. Think of pulling the core body, that is facing to the side, toward the point where the hand is grabbing the water, and

Drill name	Purpose	Description
		feel like you are going up over a barrel with your arm. Make the stroke complete by rolling to other side without lifting your head for a breath and kick on your side for a few kicks to reinforce the side streamline position. Then take a breath. Continue streamline on side position on the other side and repeat.
10-3-10 (or 6-3-6)	Balance, streamline and rolling side to side, head position, arm propulsion	Start off the same as the side kick 6-6 and instead of taking only one stroke, take three strokes while emphasizing the roll side to side in the streamline balanced position (like a log rolling) and hip drive. Breathing is preferable after the third stroke without lifting the head during the side switching in order to hold the streamline position and really feel the switch through the hips.
3 swim, 4 back	Balance, streamline, mental awareness of balance	Swim three front crawl or freestyle strokes, then roll over on back rotating around outstretched leading arm. Once on your back, take 4 back strokes, then roll over onto your stomach rotating around outstretched leading arm. Focus on keeping your balance and not dragging the legs during the roll back to the stomach.
Catch up	Balance, hip roll coordinated with arm stroke, breathing on side,	Start in the streamline position with both hands leading in front of you, touching together. Initiate the stroke with one hand while holding

Drill name	Purpose	Description
	focus on one arm catch/pull, hand entry	the other arm out in front. Return the pulling arm to "catch up" to the other arm. Allow body/hips to roll slightly in coordination with the arm stroke. After the pulling arm finishes the catch-up to the one outstretched in front, pause, relax and let your body find its natural balance position. Repeat with other arm.
Fingertip drag	Recovery for arm, correction for "wind-milling" arms	Swim regular stroke and on the recovery, pull thumb up your inseam almost to your armpit. Drag your fingers slowly toward the front entry position on the top of the water with your elbow high. Relax and move slowly for better awareness.
Hitch	Body balance and roll side to side	Swim a regular stroke and on the recovery before the arm is returned to the front entry position, reach to the back with the arm and tap the water behind the hips. This will help exaggerate the body roll.
Swim w/ kick board between legs	Balance, roll side to side, core strength	Swim with a kick board between the legs like a shark fin and focus on rolling more side to side.
One arm, with non-pulling arm in front	Balance, hip drive, one arm propulsion	Streamline kicking with hands leading position, then stroke with just one arm while breathing on the same side. Roll for the breath without lifting the head. Feel the propulsion with acceleration of the arm from the catch to the finish.
One arm, with non-pulling arm at side, breath to pulling arm side	Balance, hip drive, one arm propulsion	Streamline kicking with hands at side position, then stroke with just one arm while breathing on the same side as pulling arm.

Drill name	Purpose	Description
One arm, with non-pulling arm at side, breath to non-pulling arm side	Balance, rolling to side, one arm propulsion	Streamline kicking with hands leading position, then stroke with just one arm while breathing on the opposite side as pulling arm.
Underwater dog paddle	Catch, high elbow position, and finish for underwater part of stroke	Swim head down, kicking enough to maintain balance and extend arm in catch position. Pull through with high elbow, accelerating to the finish, but do not recover arm above the water. Instead bring it back to the front while the other arm engages in the catch, pull and finish.
Head up front crawl	Open water skill, strength with triceps	Swim with the head up and straight forward. Reach out in front, keep the elbows high on the recovery and keep the triceps pushing through hard underwater.
Power kick	Open water skill, strength with legs	Kick harder while swimming for the first half of the length, then return to regular kick.
Closed fist/ open hand	Feeling using wrists, arm surface area for pulling. High elbow through water.	Swim normally with your fists closed. Alternate lengths with hands wide open like webbed feet.
Sculling – front, mid, back	Hand position, feel for water, propulsion	Generally done face down balanced with minimal kicking, keeping arms/bent elbows into side and moving hands back and forth to "scull" and propel body forward. Hands can be positioned in front, middle, or back position of the stroke.

Open water swimming can be an exhilarating adventure or a scary nightmare for many women. This is often what holds many women back from attempting triathlon, especially at ocean venues. Fear of open water need not hold you back. You can shed your fears if you practice and develop open water skills and strategies to keep yourself calm and strong during challenges, such as turbulent starts or waves.

Factors for open water swim success include:

1. **Safety** – Know your limits. If the currents, tides, or waves are too much for you, don't hesitate to stop and seek help from the life guards on the course.
2. **Wet suits** – Use a well fitting suit to provide you with warmth and buoyancy, and more ease in the water.
3. **Skills and strategies** – Practice these so you are prepared for the challenges in open water.

Open water swim strategies:

1. Relax, relax, relax.
2. Create "your space."
3. Swim straight – Sight markers with a periodic head up check.
4. If in trouble, STOP. Breaststroke, tread water, grab a kayak or call for assistance.
5. Draft – Stay in the "bubbles" of the person in front of you.
6. Breathe on the opposite side when dealing with rough waves.

Open water swim skills to practice:

1. **Sighting/Navigation** – Once you are able to swim with effective strokes, the next most important thing in open water is that you are able to stay on course. Heading in the wrong direction can add a lot of time to your race, not to mention taking you away from the safety zone where life guards and race staff can assist you if you were to get in trouble. Being able to swim straight in open water can be facilitated by practicing your sighting and navigating. If the buoys are small or difficult to see, consider selecting some key land markers such as a tree or cliff on shore and do periodic head up checks to ensure you are heading in the appropriate direction.

An important race day consideration is to know where the sun is at the time your event. If it is going to be directly in your face at some point on the course, you would benefit from rehearsing that to be better prepared and in deciding how you will navigate the course.

2. **Eyes closed** – Another beneficial skill to practice that will help you swim straighter is to swim a few lengths in the pool, or even in the open water, with your eyes closed. When you open your eyes (if you haven't already hit the lane ropes in the pool!) you will get an idea of your tendency to go to the left or right. This may also pinpoint the need to correct part of your stroke since a dropping elbow on one side will result in a stronger stroke on the other side, thus pulling you to one direction.

   This skill may also be beneficial during your event by helping to tune out all the outside stimulus (including frightening looking water) and to remain focused on your body and breathing. There have been many triathlon races where I have had my eyes closed for much of the swim while I enjoyed getting in the "zone." Just sight every so often for a buoy to ensure you are on course.

3. **Drafting** – This is a powerful skill to master in order to take your open water swimming to a new level. Unlike cycling, drafting is permissible in the swim portion of triathlon. If you can follow close behind someone on her feet, you will swim at a faster rate with less energy. The best way to take advantage of the draft is to get behind swimmers who are able to hold a straight line and who are going slightly faster than you can on your own, then feel for the bubbles in order to stay directly in their slipstream without lifting your head to check all the time.

4. **Passing** – Know how to pass people in the open water while maintaining your stroke rhythm. You may need to give some harder kicks to get past another swimmer or watch out for her swinging arms.

5. **Creating your space** – When it gets very crowded, your swim style can become cramped and it becomes harder to relax. Don't be

afraid to "claim your space" and move your elbows a little wider than normal in order to keep your space to swim comfortably.

6. **Beach or treading water starts** – Many open water swims begin on the beach, which means you will need to run through the water before it gets deep enough for you to begin swimming. When the water becomes more than knee deep, running through the water can take up more energy than doing dolphin dives in and out. Learn to dolphin dive head first over waves and water and come up again for another dive. When the water is deep enough, you will already be in the water horizontal to start swimming.

A treading water start can be a little scary if crowded. When the gun goes, everyone moves from upright to horizontal and the chances of getting kicked are high. Learn to position yourself where you are comfortable and in line with your skill and speed. Practice finding an open line or another person to draft behind after a chaotic treading water start.

7. **Buoy turns** – Most open water swims will have buoys for you to navigate around. These turns can become very congested with a lot of swimmers slowing or becoming upright to avoid hitting others. Consider your best strategy for going around buoy turns. You may like to get close or go wide, but consider how you can take the turn efficiently and quickly without getting beaten up. Practice with your partners in a lake or crowded pool.

8. **Exits and wet suit removal** – Just because you hit the beach doesn't mean your skills for the swim portion are over. Like the entry at the start of the race, exiting the water and removing your goggles, cap and wet suit efficiently is another skill to add to your triathlon tool kit.

Practice this before your events. You will want to consider how far the transition area is from the water and wether you want to run with your wet suit on and remove in the transition area, will begin to take off while you are running to the transition, or remove your wet suit completely at the water exit and carry it with you to the transition. For some longer transitions that involve a hill climb, this might be the best strategy since the wet suit can be cumbersome to run in. Also, if your wet suit is hard to get off at the ankles, apply a little body glide around the ankles when you put on your suit. Practice this to perfection and see how quick you can get your best transition time.

BIKE LIKE LANCE

Bike handling skills

In order to have a more enjoyable and safer ride, it will help if you become comfortable on your bike, whether zipping around corners, hammering in a pace line or screaming down hills. Handle your bike well, riding any terrain or situation, and you will get more out of your training and your partners. Better bike handling skills will help you become stronger, more fit on the bike, and ready to push to new levels.

One of Malaysia's few female triathletes – Fiona Lim – on the bike at Ironman Malaysia 2005.

The first way to build good skills on a bike is to have a proper fitting bike. If the handlebars are too much of a stretch, the seat hurts you or the top tube is too high, it's going to leave you thinking more about your discomfort than your riding position and effectiveness. A comfortable seat will also help your handling skills since you will be able to sit in a relaxed manner, without shifting around or rocking your hips on the saddle.

Safety for women

Safety on your bike – The first and foremost thing to consider before you head out on your bike is safety. With little but a helmet and a layer of lycra between you and the road or much bigger vehicles, safety precautions are warranted. Consider the damage that can occur when riding at high speeds. Your life, and even the lives of those you are riding with, depends on following good safety practices:

- Never ever, ever ride without an approved helmet.
- Obey the traffic laws as you are considered a vehicle and subject to the same penalties as vehicles if you are found breaking the rules of the road.
- Watch out for dogs – there is dog spray for those who may have regular cycling routes with gnarly pets that may try to chase and scare you. Often the best way to curb them is simply loud shouting or squirting water at them.
- Headphones are extremely dangerous as you can miss hearing important noises like car horns, shouts or crashes behind you.
- Before each ride, take a minute to do a safety check of the important parts of your bike. You do not want to have a mechanical failure going down a hill at 70 kilometers per hour. See the Bike Safety Checklist below.

Bike Safety Checklist		
1. WHEELS	– pressure good	❑
	– brake distance good	❑
	– quick release tight	❑
2. BRAKES	– pressure tight	❑
	– not touching	❑
3. CRANK	– no side to side motion	❑
	– pedals spin easily	❑
4. HELMET	– tight	❑
5. SEAT	– tight	❑

Bike handling skills

Ride a straight line – This is the first important skill to master when riding a bike. Riding without weaving or erratic changes will be safer and faster since the shortest distance between two points is a straight line. Practice by riding on the white line on the road and hold your upper body relaxed and solid without any rocking back and forth on the saddle. Look forward about 10 to 15 feet to pick your line. Your eyes should also be scanning the situation around you and farther ahead in order to anticipate dangerous situations that warrant safety action or a change of course.

Cornering – Holding your line and bike strong around corners will help you ride better in groups and reduce time in races. Approach the corner a little wide, lean into the corner with your inside pedal and leg up, and press down on your outside leg or pedal and arm or handle-bar. Do not brake around the corner or come out too wide. If you need to slow down for the corner, brake before the turn. Once back upright and ready to ride a straight line, consider standing up to accelerate back up to speed faster. Practice tight turns in a parking lot, attempting to handle your bike with only one hand.

Braking – 90 percent of your braking power comes from the front brakes so use them, but if you are stopping very quickly use the front brakes together with the rear brakes. Feather your breaks for slight speed reduction when in groups to help slow down a little.

If you have clipless pedals, you will find that if you do not wish to fall over when you stop, you will need to remember to unclip and lean to the side that the curb is on. Many first-time users, however, do find that they will experience one or two falls before they remember that they need to clip out and lean to the side for their free foot to touch the pavement.

Cadence – Your skill on your bike will increase relative to your ability to spin effectively. Attempt to hold a high cadence, or revolutions per minute (rpms), in your small chain ring without bouncing. Smooth round circles are the aim in order to get the most out of the entire pedal stroke and allow your muscles to handle longer distance riding. Mashing hard in the large chain ring will tire out your muscles faster. Unless you are a 60 second sprinter, you will benefit from not pushing down hard on your pedals every stroke, but rather think of putting force on the pedal around the entire stroke. Consider kicking more forward, and using the glut and hip flexor muscles to pull the pedal up and over the top crank position.

The most optimal cadences on flat surfaces will be 85 to 90 rpms, and on hills, the range will depend on the steepness of the hill, but the cadence will be lower. Grinding at a cadence below 60 will generally not be effective during regular riding, though it can be useful for short intervals less than a minute for strength training on the bike.

You can enhance your cadence by using a cyclometer that measures cadence, or practice drills by counting with your watch in 15- or 30-second intervals and multiplying to get the per minute value. Riding down a hill and spinning as fast as you possibly can is another great way to really learn to move your legs quicker and more effectively around the pedal stroke.

When your legs become more sensitive to spinning and you don't mash your gears, you will be better able to respond to different changes of speed or direction on courses and in group riding situations.

Hill climbing – Unless you live on the plains, most riding situations will involve some kind of change in elevation and hill climbs. For the most part, your best approach to hill climbing is to spin in an easy gear and try to stay seated. Be in the proper gear when you hit the hill bottom. Watch ahead and anticipate the terrain change. If there is a downhill before the uphill, you would even benefit from gearing down and pushing the pace up so you have a bit of float at the first part of the hill before you have to start pushing harder. Make sure you are good at shifting your gears before you try this. If you don't get into the small chain ring and low gear on the back cassette fast enough, you might not be able to keep your momentum up the hill and could even fall over. This would be very hazardous in a race situation with other cyclists around.

One of the best tips for hill climbing is to count your strokes one at a time and focus on that instead of wanting to be at the top of the hill already. Also make sure you use your upstroke by pressing the heel of your foot back into the heel of the shoe and pull up with your hip flexor and hamstring muscles, giving them some extra work.

To get a little more power on the pedals, especially up short steep hills, try alternating between seated and standing positions. When standing, use your arms and pull a bit with the handlebars for some extra force. Stand with your chest open and a bit of a lean forward to get the most out of your body weight directly over the pedals. Push down and pull up. This gets the heart rate up so it may be harder, but it will get you up the hill faster in general and it uses different muscles so it can be a bit of a break from the seated position. Your bike may sway side to side – this is ok.

Do not hold onto your aerobars on the uphill climbs as this does not provide optimal stability. Also, standing over the top of a hill to get going again is a great skill to practice, as many people ease off at the top of a hill, and in a race situation you can often find the top of a hill is a place to pull away.

Different hill climbs or skills to conquer:
- Long switchback climbs
- Gradual long climbs (seated)
- Short and steep (standing)
- Down hills – tuck, squeeze knees together to make an aerodynamic position
- Big gear strength – lower cadence uphill while seated is beneficial
- Long and steep – consider using a bit of diagonal tactics, taking the hill with a zig-zag approach, rather than straight up. Do this only if it is safe or traffic free.

Tips for triathletes: Bike efficiently
- Ride with higher cadences and work on pedaling efficiency with spinning drills aiming at 90 to 100 rpms (revolutions per minute). Avoid gear mashing. Take smooth, round pedal strokes. Think kicking forward and pulling back rather than pushing down.
- Learn to ride effectively in your small chain ring.
- Ride with "middle" gearing, not at the extremes on your back cassette.
- Be still and relaxed on your saddle – your hips should not rock around as you pedal.

- Hold a straight line.
- Avoid holding on to your aeropads – unless they are designed for that.
- Unless you are in the lead, avoid riding in your aerobars in groups.
- Dress appropriately – in tight, aerodynamic clothing, not with flapping t-shirts.
- Keep your equipment clean and well oiled.
- Have your helmet fitted tight.
- Lean in with pressure on your outside pedal and handlebar to handle your cornering line comfortably.
- Don't litter gel or sport bar packets.

Group riding

Safety with group riding depends first and foremost on good communication and no radical or unannounced changes in your riding. It can be dangerous if you weave or don't know how to appropriately communicate. Be very verbal and loud with your calls and cues when in a group, and signal well to those rides behind you. Some tips for riding safely and effectively in a group are included below.

Effective group riding skills:
- Pay attention – monitor riders in front, to the side and behind, and watch for hazards in the road condition, such as potholes, glass, or gravel. Keep an eye out for moving traffic or parked cars, especially if a driver is about to open a door!
- Focus on the saddle area of the rider in front of you and watch for the brakes being used.
- Have good communication about traffic warnings, road hazards, turns and speed changes.
- Stay steady – consistent riding is key to riding safely in a group.
- Make subtle changes – avoid braking suddenly or turning radically.
- Stay in close formation with the pack so you don't break the pace line.
- Try to relax when other riders get close to you. Stay balanced and in control of your bike.
- Take your turn as the lead person taking pulls.
- When you take the lead, maintain a pace and don't try to drop the pack.

- Keep paired in a two-bike pace line for most rides, unless the road is too narrow or busy.
- Ask for help if you are getting dropped.
- Have courtesy for fellow riders.
- Avoid riding with headphones.
- Know your strengths and weaknesses and work as a team with other riders so no one gets left behind.
- Know if/when you are going to be a hazard (due to fitness or riding skills) and drop back or be in a position in the pack that makes you less hazardous to other riders.

Aerobars – NEVER get in your aerobars in a pack when you are following in the middle of the group. It's ok for the lead woman, but highly inappropriate, dangerous and disrespectful to the group riders behind you. Generally, in a less experienced group your hands should be poised over the brakehoods or fingers relaxed on the levers. In more experienced groups, I'll trust riding with my hands in my drops (bottom part of the handlebars) if there is a strong headwind or it is hammertime. If I am sitting up and leisurely spinning and enjoying the draft, I will relax them on the top of the handlebars.

Lastly, if there is considerable hill riding, this can cause a little more challenge when riding in a group because cyclists will have varying degrees of hill climbing ability based on strength, fitness and, in the case of newbies, shifting knowledge. It can be a little scary when there is a big power drop from the woman in front of you as you hit a steep incline and her wheel is coming back at you fast. So coming up on ascents, the red alert should come on and, for a less experienced group, more space should be allowed between riders to accommodate for the differences in climbing. Wheel rubbing can happen pretty fast on a climb if someone jumps out of the saddle or drops back to his/her seat.

Communications in groups:
- **Right turns** are signaled by pointing with your right arm and yelling, „right". Do the same but with your left arm for left turnes. You need to be very vocal in a group to communicate what's going on so that those at the back can follow appropriately and not crash into you.

- **To signal stopping or slowing** place your hand, palm facing back on your lower butt just above your saddle, and yell, "slowing" or "stopping" so everyone behind you knows you're slowing or putting on the brakes. Think of it like your brake lights. The best place to put the hand is right around the saddle/butt area because it will be directly in view of the person behind you.

- **Road obstacles** up ahead warrant communication by pointing to the ground and yelling, "pot hole" or "glass" or whatever the obstacle is so that everyone can be forewarned (you won't see these things when you are following in a group). This is critical to ensure that those in the back of the group ride safely.

- **Vehicles on the road** require extra attention and notification to the group. If you are in the rear and a car is coming, you should yell, "car back" to warn those in front of you of the impending pass by a vehicle and the need to move more to the right. If you are at the front and on a narrow road in a double pace line, and there is a car coming in the opposite direction, you should yell, "car up".

- **Intersections** can be dangerous if you don't take the time to check for vehicles. If you are going through an intersection, look both ways and, if safe, yell, "Clear" these.

Drafting

When there is a rider in front of you, you are able to go at the same speed with less energy because there is less resistance. The energy savings can be around 15%. That is why it is not legal in an individual time trial (TT) race in cycling or a triathlon, which is intended to be an individual race. Drafting, however, is allowed in the professional ranks. Thus team work becomes important. Amateurs can still benefit from training that involves drafting.

What draft?

Even though drafting is not allowed in age-group triathlon, I recommend still learning to draft in group situations. Riding a pace line (straight line) or echelon (staggered line), in which you rotate leads, is an excellent way to learn to focus on good form and faster riding.

1. Efficiency leads to greater endurance opportunities for training and improved racing performance by using less energy for biking.
2. Drafting results in riding farther on less work thus building your neuromuscular endurance.
3. Helps enhance your bike handling skills and confidence and comfort on a bike.
4. Learn how to feel a faster pace.
5. There is more safety for groups in a draft pace line than in random formation on road.

When you take your turn at the lead, it's important that you keep a steady speed and not try to pull away from the pack or slow down. If you are new to group riding and close drafting, try getting comfortable just riding in the back and only take your turn to pull at the front when you are comfortable. When you pull off to the side after leading, try to stay close to the pack so that when the final rider comes by, it is easier to jump behind her and stay in the draft zone or slipstream.

Once you lose contact with a pack and the slipstream, or draft, it is harder to catch up again. Another important thing in groups is not to use your brakes too much or weave around.

Bike adjustments and assembly

Becoming an empowered independent tri woman includes being able to handle your bike both while on the road and on trips to racing venues.

I recommend learning how to do the following on your own:
- fix a tire
- lube and clean your chain
- adjust the brakes
- take apart and pack for traveling
- doing all of this with your own tools

I try to empower my athletes to be able to handle their bike issues themselves and not feel like they need a mechanic to do it. Self reliance builds self-confidence. It's your choice if you want to spend the money on assembling but its good to have the skill to put your bike together on your own. Besides, it's nice to know you've put it all together and tightened everything and know when you are riding it's not going to fall apart on you.

If you think it is too complicated, consider what one of my athletes had to say about learning to take apart her own bike before a recent overseas trip to her first Ironman. "It's much easier than I thought it would be. I am going to practice putting it back together when I get home and then have the mechanic check it out to make sure everything is as it should be. I wanted someone to teach me and didn't want to do this 'unsupervised' for the first time. Don't worry – my plan is to do it all on my own for Ironman."

Bike disassembly in 10 quick steps

Traveling to races where you need to fly requires you to disassemble and pack your bike into a bike box. As a veteran of this process, I've learned to do it rather quickly and even timed myself. My record is seven minutes from riding to fully boxed – motivated by the cab driver waiting in my driveway to take me to the airport.

Order of disassembly for me (you may wish to devise your own routine order):

1. Take off wheels (30 seconds)
2. Take skewers out of hubs (45 seconds) (so that they don't protrude through the cardboard box)
3. Take pedals off with wrench (1 minute)
4. Take seat post out with allen key (30 seconds)
5. Take off aerobars with allen key (1-2 minutes depending on set up and bolts used)
6. Loosen head set or handlebars to be able to turn them to fit the box you have (30 seconds to 1 minute)
7. Put frame in box and surround with padding, towels, etc. (1-2 minute)
8. Put wheels in box and surround with padding, etc. (<1 minute)
9. Throw in your running shoes, helmet, water bottles, cycling shoes, bike pump, seat, pedals, etc. (30 seconds)
10. Close box with straps or use a cardboard box seal with packing tape and reinforce with duct tape (45 seconds). Reinforce as needed at airport while standing in line. No need to waste time!

Over the years, I probably could have been more careful with packing and protecting my frame – I've had a couple times where it has been scratched unnecessarily. I also know to add extra layers of cardboard on the bottom where the chain ring rests if I have cardboard box. Other hard case boxes, such as Trico or Trisport, have padding inside the box and straps to hold wheels in place. The benefit of these boxes is that they also have wheels on the bottom for easy pulling in the airport.

RUN LIKE A GAZELLE

Efficient running form

Excellence in sports movement is achieved through efficient form. Effortlessness. Flow. Graceful. Smooth. Whatever you want to call it.

For experienced or natural runners who have been running effortlessly for years, there is no need to think twice about form and cadence.

Good form comes from being relaxed while moving your body with good biomechanics. Your efficiency will be improved with a relaxed posture, and even more by

Darlene Hall shows fine form at Ironman USA in Lake Placid, New York in 2005.

consistent breathing patterns, enabling you to run with maximal force output for longer periods of time with less energy than if you had poor posture and poor breathing. This is especially challenging and critical in triathlon where the running leg follows swimming and cycling and your muscles and mental focus are already fatigued.

Body form checklist

Consider a head-to-toe body scan of your running posture while you run or do form drills. There are a number of form drills that can help you increase your awareness of your body position, and build your agility and leg strength. A list of form drills will follow later in this chapter.

Head – Look ahead in a neutral position. Try to think of centering your head with your ears over your shoulders and extending your spine through the top of your head.

Shoulders – Hold your shoulders open and relaxed, and watch that they don't round forward. You want the chest open so you can get full breaths into the lungs. Being hunched over is a strain also for your back muscles.

Arms – Hold your arms relaxed, with elbows bent and close to your side when swinging alongside your body, not crossing over or swinging wide. Keep everything moving in a straight line from your elbows to your hands.

Hands – Hands should be relaxed and loosely cupped, not closed fists, with palms facing each other.

Pelvis and hips – Your body should be centered over the pelvis and not bent forward. Though a slight lean forward helps keep you to use gravity to move to the next stride. Your power and balance comes from your pelvic area. This is why having a strong core to hold straight posture is important to strong running. A weak core or hamstrings can result in running with a forward lean or an inability to pull the hips underneath you. Closed eye drills standing on one leg will help teach you more about the balance and power center in the pelvis.

Legs – Move forward with your knees facing straight ahead and not extending stride more than natural. Think of someone attaching a string to your kneecaps and pulling your knees forward with each stride.

Feet – Consider a midfoot impact, rather than a ball of the foot or a heel strike. Planting your foot directly under the body and your center of gravity will be most efficient for endurance running and help keep you injury free. The impact on and placement of your feet is one of the first places to investigate when an injury in the lower limbs develops.

One of the most popular skill-based approaches for running is called the Pose Method. To learn more, check out the book titled *Pose Method of Running* published by Dr. Nicholas Romanov in 2002. The website www.posetech.com provides other resources and information on clinics or coaches around the world who instruct the technique.

Breathing

Fluid form will begin with a relaxed body that comes from being able to breathe with a smooth rhythm while relaxed, even when the intensity increases. Exhale fully through your nose and mouth in order to then fully inhale. Breathe deep breaths, down to your belly, not short breaths from your chest. Deep and deliberate relaxed breathing will help you deal with cramps. To establish more awareness and control of your breathing, it is worth trying some laps around the track or on a smooth trail where you breathe only through your nose.

The goal is to eventually run smoothly and steadily without thinking of your form. However, at the end of races that you are feeling very fatigued you will often benefit from thinking of your posture and breathing.

Running cadence

Running cadence is something that few think about when they run, but many could benefit from doing more effectively. For many women, especially beginners or those slightly overweight, huge benefits will come from concentrating on keeping your turnover in an effective range.

Why is cadence important? Ever watch the back of the pack of a 5k? Most folks lop along at maybe 75 or 80 cadence cycles a minute. The first thing a beginner can do, besides have good posture, is to increase her turnover to an effective rate. For experienced runners it's not usually an issue, though I know when I'm struggling in a short race like a 5k, turnover will be the first thing I try to focus on to get back on pace. It takes mental practice before it becomes more natural all the time.

To understand faster running, consider that speed in running is a simple math equation.

Physics of Speed = Stride Rate (SR) x Stride Length (SL)

Stride length is dependent on the amount force applied by your foot/muscles against the ground and will be affected by forces in the opposing direction (i.e. your weight – which is relative to gravity, your strength, or wind against you). From a mathematical perspective, improving speed comes with:

1. Faster cadence (SR)
2. Losing weight (SL)
3. Getting stronger (SL)
4. Drafting (if windy) (SL)
5. Flexible muscles for good range of motion (SL)

While they do have running metronomes to count your strides for the low-tech, budget-minded woman like me, I just use my watch.

I like to count cycles, so I just keep track of left foot counts (or right foot if you wish), and do it with my countdown timer on my watch set at 30 seconds repeat, then just listen for the beep (this works better when you are running in the dark). So I'll have 30 seconds "on" counting and aim for 45-48 (i.e., 90-96 cycles, or 180-188 foot strikes), and 30 seconds "off" just trying to hold the feeling, and repeat. Increasing cadence comes easier if you think of "quick feet" lifting off the ground with little contact time. Sometimes in the middle of a long run, I'll insert a few cadence checks for 5 minutes to remind me to keep focused on my light effective turnover and keep the neural pathways in tune.

Running form drills

Form drills – These can be incorporated into workouts at the end of short runs or at the beginning of track speed workouts. Select 4 to 6 drills to repeat and cover 40-50 meters and walk back. The aim is to emphasize the form, such as high knee, quick feet and tall posture, rather than to cover a lot of ground.

- High knee skips – exaggerate the knee lift action while skipping off the ball of the foot and swinging the arms opposite to the knee lifting.
- Rear heel kicks – exaggerate the heel lift action by attempting to kick the heels of your feet up to your butt while swimming
- Backward skipping – exaggerate the knee lift action while skipping backwards

- Side skips – face sideways and shuffle along bringing both legs in together at the same time and then out again while keeping straight posture
- Agility vine – face sideways and quickly step one leg to cross over the other, and then cross behind the other and repeat. When you get better at this, you can lift your knees higher.
- Balance pose with lunges – balance on one foot with the knee lifted in front in the run position and lunge lifted leg forward to transfer weight, then come up to balance pose position and repeat the lunge. Swing arm opposite to knee lifted.
- Strides – accelerate to full speed striding with good form

Other form reminders below can be repeated on a longer run or during laps around a track:

- breathing through nose
- cadence 30 second cycles
- eyes closed
- arm swings and chest openers
- relaxed arms
- stiff straight arms
- hands on head
- straight leg run
- barefoot strides

Hill form drills

These drills will help you prepare for better hill running both physically and mentally. They are best done on a moderate steady grade hill for a duration of 30 to 45 seconds with a walk between repeats. These will help strengthen the muscles for hill running and allow you to find your best hill running technique.

- Vertical form – run uphill with exaggerated leg lift vertically and exaggerated arm swing
- Horizontal form – run uphill with exaggerated leg stride horizontally and exaggerated arm swing
- Quick feet form – run uphill with very quick turnover and small steps uphill

- Downhill strides – lean into the hill to allow gravity to carry you and let your heels kick up behind you. Don't try to brake with the front legs or you will put undue strain on your knees. Downhill running on trails requires very strong, stable ankles. Consider ankle stability exercises before attempting fast downhill run strides.

CHAPTER 6
Mental Skills for Tri Women

Like any muscle in your body, your brain is also an organ that can be trained and developed to enhance its neural pathways. When it comes to triathlon, mastering mental skills can make or break your performance, and more importantly, your joy for the experience. Many women don't realize how important their minds are in creating their perspective of the experience. Where your mind goes, the body follows; thus your mind can make or break you. Attitude is 90 percent of it.

Using your mind skillfully will enhance your triathlon experience both in training and racing. Taking time to develop mental strategies such as goal setting, and practice specific mental skills such as visualizations, will help make the most of your training time and racing opportunities.

The importance of goal setting was discussed in Chapter Two, but is worth mentioning again. If you wish to drive to a particular destination, having a detailed road map and planned route will certainly help with the trip. Otherwise, you could waste a great deal of time lost on the road.

Many women often overlook setting mental goals and putting the time into training the mind. Start with an assessment of your mental skills such as the Assessment of Psychological Skills on the following pages, which was taken from the USAT coaching manual. Once a few areas of weakness have been identified, consider short-term and long-term goals to improve them.

The skills that seem to be the most challenging for women, especially those who begin triathlon as adults without a background of competitive sports, are competitive anxiety, self-criticism/perfectionism, race intelligence, confidence, and emotional stability.

Pre-race anxiety is best tackled by three mental strategies –
- **Relaxation techniques** (such as deep breathing, progressive muscle relaxation, soothing music)
- **Developing a detailed race plan**, which includes pacing decisions, positive self-talk or mantras and nutrition details. Extra pre-race calm and confidence can be ensured by developing contingency plans with how you will deal with various challenges, such as a flat tire or bike crash. Consider how you physically and mentally deal with all these issues and calmly accept those things that are out of your control such, as weather or traffic.
- **Visualization techniques** where you picture yourself going through the triathlon swim, bike and run with power and perfect form. Practicing visualizations can happen prior to training, on rest days or even during key workouts.

In Terri Schneider's recent book *The Triathlete's Guide to Mental Training,* she thoroughly discusses developing emotional mastery for triathlon with respect to the emotional challenges of fear, frustration, despair and post-race depression.

An important point she makes about post-race depression, a common affliction for endurance athletes following a big event where you feel down and with little energy, is not to avoid it, but to "learn how to deal with this uncomfortable post-event experience." She advises to accept it as a normal and necessary part of triathlon that plays a vital role in your complete recovery and eventual rejuvenation, not just at a physical level but also on a psychological and emotional level. Thus, acceptance of this process of renewal and acknowledgement of these uncomfortable feelings that will pass in time, are important skills to have in your mental tool box.

Two other great books on mental training recommended for reading include Terry Orlick's *Psyching for Sport: Mental Training for Athletes*

(1986) and JoAnn Dahlkoetter's *Your Performing Edge: The Complete Mind-Body Guide for Excellence in Sports, Health and Life*.

Assessment of Psychological Skills (from USAT Level 2 Manual)

Assess your psychological skills using the following rating scale

1 (low)   2   3   4   5   6   7   8   9   10   (high)

	1	2	3	4	5	6	7	8	9	10
1. Commitment to Training	1	2	3	4	5	6	7	8	9	10
2. Commitment to Specific areas of improvement	1	2	3	4	5	6	7	8	9	10
3. Motivation	1	2	3	4	5	6	7	8	9	10
4. Distraction Control	1	2	3	4	5	6	7	8	9	10
5. Concentration (sustained focus)	1	2	3	4	5	6	7	8	9	10
6. Competitive Anxiety Control (cognitive and somatic)	1	2	3	4	5	6	7	8	9	10
7. Mental Toughness (aggressiveness, persistence, determination)	1	2	3	4	5	6	7	8	9	10
8. Controlling Negative Emotions (anger, frustration)	1	2	3	4	5	6	7	8	9	10
9. Confidence in Ability	1	2	3	4	5	6	7	8	9	10
10. Confidence Under Pressure	1	2	3	4	5	6	7	8	9	10
11. Mental Rehearsal Abilities	1	2	3	4	5	6	7	8	9	10
12. Attention (shifting of focus)	1	2	3	4	5	6	7	8	9	10
13. Relaxation Skills	1	2	3	4	5	6	7	8	9	10
14. Goal setting (short, intermediate and long-term)	1	2	3	4	5	6	7	8	9	10
15. Self-criticism/Perfectionism	1	2	3	4	5	6	7	8	9	10
16. Dealing with Fatigue	1	2	3	4	5	6	7	8	9	10
17. Dealing with Pain	1	2	3	4	5	6	7	8	9	10

18. Self care (sleep, eating, recovery, injury prevention)   1 2 3 4 5 6 7 8 9 10

19. Relations with Team (providing support)   1 2 3 4 5 6 7 8 9 10

20. Relations with Coach (asking for feedback and clarification)   1 2 3 4 5 6 7 8 9 10

21. Family Relations (approval, resentments, self-esteem)   1 2 3 4 5 6 7 8 9 10

22. Memory of Feedback from Coach   1 2 3 4 5 6 7 8 9 10

23. Execution of Feedback   1 2 3 4 5 6 7 8 9 10

24. Ability to Change   1 2 3 4 5 6 7 8 9 10

25. Risk Taking   1 2 3 4 5 6 7 8 9 10

26. Controlling Intensity (calm or active self)   1 2 3 4 5 6 7 8 9 10

27. Training Intensity   1 2 3 4 5 6 7 8 9 10

28. Race Intelligence   1 2 3 4 5 6 7 8 9 10

Chose three areas in which you would like to improve and provide three steps on how to improve each mental skill. Set a deadline to re-assess the psychological skills you chose to improve.

1. a.
   b.
   c.

2. a.
   b.
   c.

3. a.
   b.
   c.

If you are truly looking for a breakthrough in your training and triathlon performances, don't skip the all-important development of your mental muscle. Not only will your results soar but your enjoyment for the sport will increase. This is a healthy, holistic approach for women, which brings balance to the mind, body and spirit.

Darlene Hall at Ironman USA in Lake Placid, New York in 2005

As former professional triathlete Brad Kearns writes in his recent book *Breakthrough Triathlon Training*:

"A champion athlete is someone who is skilled and balanced not only physically, but mentally and emotionally. Champion athletes train and race extremely hard, but they also have a tremendous ability to back off when they need to, stay positive after defeat and disappointment, and be flexible in their thoughts and actions. They have an honest and sincere commitment to their peak performance goals that is more powerful than ego demands, personal insecurities, and the lure of the unhealthy, sedentary modern world.

Champions are able to maintain physical, mental and emotional health in pursuit of fitness."

Competitive triathlon women should heed Kearns' words – results happen naturally when motivation is pure and you pursue your goals with a genuine love for training, competition, and the opportunity to grow as a person through your athletic challenges. While victories, paychecks or proving yourself worthy of the title "Ironman" might seem like solid sources of motivation, Kearns calls them "superficial" when compared to the higher ideals that can drive you.

If you are true to what is best for a balanced mind-body-spirit approach, you will reap the full experience and enjoyment possible from the sport.

Kearns emphasizes his point further:

"Cultivating a pure motivation will help you enjoy performance breakthroughs far beyond current levels; experience less stress, tension, and anxiety related to competition; experience less fatigue from your training regimen; and enjoy your athletics on a deeper level than ever before."

PART 3
Get Involved

CHAPTER 7
Becoming Part of the Triathlon Community

Although great attention is given to the performance and results of triathlon, women can experience more enjoyment in the sport when they fully embrace the social benefits. A sense of belonging to the triathlon community through strong friendships, training partners, or club teammates will create a supportive environment that can boost your enthusiasm, and ultimately help you have better races. Happy, fulfilled athletes perform better. And, even if you don't perform well by your standards, if you have friends and colleagues within the triathlon community, you will still have people to cheer you on, encourage you, challenge you or, better yet, share a finish line hug or a post-race drink with!

It might take a bit of effort, but you will reap far more than you sow in this area. Developing rewarding social connections in triathlon is part of the mind-body-spirit approach to the sport that women can benefit from. A balanced sportswoman will seek more from the sport than a fit physique, medals and PR (personal record) achievements. The suggestions in this chapter provide guidance on how to become part of the triathlon community and enjoy more than the physical aspects of the sport.

The triathlon family – Once you finish a triathlon, you become "initiated" into the community and triathletes are often so friendly, open and welcoming to newcomers that it can be like joining a family. Those who complete the Ironman distance are typically said to now be part of the "Ironhood." It's like a brotherhood (or sisterhood) of very fit people from many walks of life. Their backgrounds may be very different, but they all share a passion for doing 140.6 miles of swim, bike and run!

Building friendships – By far one the greatest pleasures I have experienced with triathlon is the friendships I have built with so many wonderful people all over the world. You may enter the sport to become more fit, lose some weight or have a new challenge in your life, but if you are open to the friendships that come with the triathlon package, you will share your newfound fitness, achievements, or even low moments with the family of friendly triathletes around you.

Take the time to bond at races and share stories, trials and tribulations, as well as celebrate successes. Consider including in your race goals a social achievement of meeting one or two new people each race, or giving a few compliments to other women, or if you are shy, a simple smile will do wonders to make other people and yourself feel great. Open new doors for communication beyond the races by exchanging email addresses or phone numbers. You never know what might happen, if only you just make the first step to invite another tri woman friend into your life.

Encourage other women, too – whether with a thumbs up, or a "way to go" or "looking good" as you pass each other on the course in races or competitive training situations – it's healthy for even the most competitive woman to respect her competitors.

Consider your local triathlon club a great avenue to meet people, especially the club meetings and social hours. If you find yourself always training by yourself, you might consider joining a coached training group or clinic to expand your horizons physically and socially. Other places to find tri-minded women who are also internet savvy include online triathlon communities and forums, such as slowtwitch.com, trinewbies.com, club message boards, race chatlines or various coaches forums.

The friendships you make in triathlon will be precious and provide some great opportunities for adventure, especially if you travel to far away races. One of my most memorable races overseas involved sharing the journey with one of my triathlon sisters. You can read more in the story "Fit Friends, Tri for Life" on the following page.

Finding and enjoying training partners – Training partners can be found in a variety of places like races, triathlon clubs, group training sessions, online communities, fitness centers, or even out on the trail. You never know how you will meet your next training buddy!

You may even want to try posting a wanted ad for a training partner. Consider posting one in your multisport or running club newsletter or chatline, or on the bulletin board at the recreation center or fitness club.

Fit Friends, Tri for Life – Lisa Lynam

I was ocean kayaking on the Abel Tasman Sea above the south island of New Zealand in March 2000 with an Irongirlfriend from Canada. We had just finished Ironman New Zealand a few days earlier. We were reminiscing about the joys of life, such as camping on the beach in foreign lands and doing triathlons. She suggested that we come back and do this again when we were 80. I was 30 at the time and found thinking ahead just one year a challenge; even though I'm game for challenges and want to remain fit and strong for the rest of my life, the idea of planning ahead fifty years was slightly daunting. Thinking I was slightly wiser (and feeling the effects of aging more) than my youthful 24-year-old friend with boundless energy, I worked her down to age 70.

We've gone on to live in different cities and she has a family of her own, but we still keep in touch. Every so often we remind each other about 2040. Thinking I'll need to be fit and healthy enough to do an Ironman at age 70 often helps me keep things into perspective. I want to make it to that finish line, not just the ones I am trying for this year.

We'll see what the future holds, but it will be great if my girlfriend and I can travel across the Pacific Ocean and replicate our year 2000 trip. We'll do a three-day kayak trip, which will be preceded by a 10-hour hike across the Torongo Crossing, including an ascent up 7000 feet to the edge of a live steaming volcano. We might skip the skydive out of a plane at 9,000 feet, but 140.6 miles of swim, bike and run to complete the Ironman New Zealand triathlon will be a must! Having a friend to share the dream with keeps me inspired and hopeful.

Of course, she still talked me into a sprint triathlon at age 80!

Enjoy the chance to bond with your training partner – but find someone you will be comfortable with because a long session can become agonizing if you like to be silent or like to chat up a storm while training but your partner doesn't. Your training partners can be valuable motivators to keep you accountable and showing up to those workouts you may otherwise skip.

Other Social Opportunities:
- local triathlon or running club free social events (membership benefits)
- bike shops – you never know who you will meet in the repair section
- group training with a team
- post-workout breakfasts
- volunteer at races
- bond with others at special guest lectures or instructional clinics
- take time to visit people at Expo booths for local marathon or larger triathlon races
- attend pre- and post-race meals or banquets

Race organizations, club boards or other committees – Consider volunteering to be part of the organizing team for an upcoming race in your community, be on the board for your club, or find other committees that support areas of interest, and dive in! You will meet new people, gain new skills, and enhance your involvement in the sport. By participating as a race organizer, you also get to view the sport of triathlon from a different perspective and it will help you appreciate all the hard work that goes into putting on any kind of event.

When you do races yourself you will have a more genuine gratitude for the hard working volunteers and the tireless thankless job the race director has.

Becoming part of a race committee or even devising your own event can be a great way to get more immersed in the community, work as a team on a worthwhile project, and meet the many people who support the sport, such as local merchants and sponsors. When the event is in support of a special charity, you will feel that you have done something not only for the athletes and the sport, but others in need.

Research indicates that we live longer when we are able to reach out to help others and contribute beneficially to society. Many studies have proven that volunteering and charitable actions are good for our health and longevity.

In 2000, while training for another Ironman race, I dreamed up a new race event during my many century bike rides in the Texas Hill country. It was hard to believe what started as a tiny thought in mid-July became a full-fledged reality nine months later with over 600 people – participants, volunteers, supporters and spectators – gathering at the local community center for the first ever all-women's duathlon in the U.S. A year later, I produced three events, including the world's first all-women's adventure race, with over 500 women participating in the series. Directing the MultiSportswomen Series meant some of the hardest work I've ever done – doing another Ironman would have been much easier, I can assure you, but knowing I was making a positive difference in the lives of hundreds of women was incredibly fulfilling. Many of the individuals from the team I worked with are still good friends today, and hundreds of the women touched by this event have gone on to do more races. Some have completed an Ironman triathlon, or even two! Many of the women have received benefits far beyond that of a finisher's medal – they have lost weight, involved their families in more healthy living and fitness, and gained a new perspective on life. This was my way of taking my involvement in the sport to another level and experiencing the spirit of the sport at its fullest.

That kind of commitment is not for everyone, but there may be something small that you can sink your teeth into that will give you more grounding in the sport of triathlon and more enjoyment from a mind-body-spirit approach.

Take a minute to write down a couple ways you could be more involved in the sport, or meet new people who will increase your passion to participate in triathlon.

Get a new view of the sport – If you are a veteran of the sport and your tri life seems rather routine and ho-hum, consider doing something completely different and new to spice things up. Possibilities include:
• Starting from the very back of the pack and going at the pace of the slower or newer triathletes

- Wearing a funny or entertaining costume and see how many people you can make laugh
- Using a bike that is different and fun, such as a cruiser bike, or add streamers and a horn and honk as you pass people
- Volunteering to be the official last place finisher of a women-only event

The Joys of Finishing Last – Lisa Lynam

If you were to eavesdrop on a crowd of women getting ready to do their first triathlon, amongst the nervous chatter, you would probably hear something like, "I just don't want to come last." It's a fear that keeps many women away from the sport. Real or not, the thought of finishing last instills a great deal of pre-race anxiety in many female first-timers.

I have to admit, as an experienced triathlete, I didn't revel in those moments when I got my butt kicked so badly the organizers had almost dismantled the entire finish line by the time I had arrived. And having a police car cruise behind me with those red lights spinning around wasn't exactly calming either! Still, I can remember a few times when finishing last was really fun.

Like Sally Edwards at the Danskin Women's Triathlons, I've volunteered to be the official last place finisher at the Women's Triathlon in Canada and twice at the Speedo Women's Triathlon in Sugarland, Texas. Race director Andy Stewart allowed me to bring up the rear and provide women at the back of the pack with encouragement. It can be a lot of fun to be among the back of the pack because you start to really understand just how big a deal it is to simply finish. Trophies and winner's plaques are unimportant. Crossing the finish line is a momentous occasion.

Though media may focus on the race winners, most women are playing their own winning game. Injuries, illness, work and family obligations may be considerable challenges for these "everyday athletes," so the courage and determination it takes to bring up the rear, and persevere hours after the first woman has crossed the line and finished her post-race refreshments is admirable and inspiring.

- Race with a family member or friend and cross the finish line together
- Try a relay with friends or someone new to the sport
- Attempt an off-road event or an adventure race
- Lose all your devices – race without a heart rate monitor, speedometer or a watch!
- If you have children, take them to a triathlon to watch or do the race themselves
- If you don't have children, take your friend's or neighbor's kids to a kids' triathlon

Kiki Rutowski and her fiancé-now husband Scott Silver enjoy sharing the triathlon experience together.

Get your family, significant other, and friends involved

Consider that your family, spouse, boyfriend or friends may enjoy the chance to be involved, even if it is as cheerleaders from the sidelines. It will likely deepen your relationship and bring you new respect and appreciation for one another.

When Austin's Bobby Rigg signed up for her first duathlon she was persistent. She talked her mother, Mayra Holden, into doing the event. Holden, a non-exerciser, admitted she was scared and nervous before the start, but the duathlon was a memorable experience for both her and her daughter.

"When my daughter mentioned the duathlon to me, I wondered 'What the heck is that?' She then explained to me what it was and after hearing that it was for a charity, and about all the little girls that would benefit, I thought, 'Well good for you.' I was so proud of my daughter for doing this. Then she asked me if I would do it with her. My first response was, 'I can't.' After some time, my daughter talked me into it," said Holden.

Holden didn't let a sparse training regimen stop her from joining her daughter in Austin for the special experience. "We spent the day

Kiki Rutowski and her fiancé-now husband Scott Silver share a moment at the finish line.

before the race preparing, buying clothes, bike gear, and getting our bikes ready. We had a lot of fun that day. As I went to bed that night, I told my husband I was scared and nervous and didn't know if I could do it or not ... the morning of the race, I was nervous, but my daughter was with me, and everything was okay."

After almost three hours of walking, running and biking, Holden crossed the line with her daughter at her side cheering loudly. Holden persisted proudly to the finish despite heat distress.

"We finished next to last, but we all crossed the finish line together. It was one of the most happy days of my life. Considering the time spent with my daughter and that it went to benefit the girls of Liv in the Game (a charity to support girls in sport), you bet I'd do the duathlon any day!"

Holden continued to train on her own for other races to the delight of her daughter. Rigg said, "Now my mom is interested in my exercise and always asks how my rides are going. And she even gives me her own news on how she did four miles riding around the neighborhood. I am so proud of my mom. I had to force her to do the duathlon. I never dreamed my mom could be like this."

This story is just one shining example of how a little effort can reap great rewards beyond the physical aspect of triathlon.

Ironmate survival guide – for the men

Clearly, no success, even in an individual sport like triathlon, happens without a back-up team. For the more competitive age-group triathletes, particularly those competing in Ironman distance triathlons, their spouses, or significant others on the home front, may view the trip with tepid enthusiasm. Lonely Saturdays, overflowing laundry, empty fridges, overtime child-minding, extra massage requests and/or relentless pre-dawn alarms are a few of the things to "look forward to" for the mate of a dedicated Ironwoman.

For the spouses of Susanne Davis, third in her 30-34 age-group at the 2005 World Ironman Championships, and six-time World Champion and record holder Cherie Gruenfeld, third in 2005, their own performances, both on the race course and on the journey to the race, make a difference. All too often we hear stories of how the Ironman causes grief and potential divorces in relationships, but these two

Suzanne Davis at the 2005 Ironman World Championships with husband Scott and her 2-year-old son.

exceptional ultra supporters highlight how the experience can be enjoyable, and even a potentially life changing experience, for those in the supporting role.

Cherie's husband, Lee Gruenfeld, has more Ironmating experience than anyone on the lava fields in Hawaii – he has gone 17 rounds at the World Championships to refine his viewing, crowd fighting and cheering strategies. His wisdom also goes beyond managing race day strategies or juggling training schedules.

"The answer to the question of triathlon widowhood doesn't lie in logistics. It isn't about scheduling appointments with each other or apportioning the household tasks or ensuring parity or fairness or equality. It's about first realizing that, if your loved one aspires to be a triathlete, and especially one of the long-distance variety, you are linked to someone extraordinary and should be mindful of the privilege you've been afforded. You need to trust me on this one: when you see his/her face as he/she crosses the line, your life will change forever," wrote Gruenfeld in a 1999 article for *Competitor* magazine titled "A Word to the Triathlon Widow(er)."

If you're looking to involve your partner in your long and arduous Ironman journey, then consider developing a "survival strategy."

A first-time Ironmate supporter, Suzanne's husband Scott Davis, created some "team tactics" that resulted in victory both in Hawaii and

on the homefront in his relationship with his wife and two-year-old son. "For us, it was all about the family goal – get mom to the finish line," said Davis, a former Ironman California finisher himself. "Our experience was filled with pride and excitement, from the long Saturday rides to our surprise send-off party, the family reached our goal, like we do most things, together."

Suzanne Davis accepts her 3rd place prize at the 2005 Ironman World Championships with husband Scott.

Davis shares his secrets for significant-other success, better known as "a father's guide to Ironman survival":

- Develop the goal together and make a plan. Just like a business plan, an Ironman requires a plan. Make sure the family has shared agreements and roles/responsibilities are clearly defined.
- Listen. The plan will have ups and downs. Make sure you are there for the downs.
- Hire a cleaning service. There's little doubt the house could be a mess without mom around.
- Rub the feet every night. (Without her having to ask, guys.)
- Time with a two-year-old could be tough. I looked at it as a chance to really bond with my son and get to know his personality better.
- Nap when he naps. You'll need it.
- We hired a sitter for a lot of the longer rides, which allowed us to ride together and kept me in shape, too.

- Let it go. Not everything is going to get done the way it does at other times during the year. Face it, the cars may be dirty and the wash a little overflowing, but it really doesn't matter, it's only temporary.
- The little things count. Making mom a sandwich after a run or ride goes a long way. She won't forget it when it's your birthday.
- Keep your priorities. Susanne did her long runs and we still made it to church on Sunday.
- Have a reward. When everyone was leaving Kona, our Mai Tai vacation at the Marriott was just starting. Spend a week unwinding and reconnecting after the race, not a week together being stressed before the race.
- Be proud. In one of our early rides, someone asked me if my ego took a hit because my wife could out-bike me. (Actually, out-run and out-swim me, as well). NO! Be proud of your wife and her accomplishments. The gifts she has for the Ironman are the same energetic gifts she brings to the family! Now it's my turn. Susanne motivated me to do my own Half-Ironman in March.

More women Iron supporters inspired
Though most athletes look to their coaches, doctors or massage therapists to boost their performance, many age-group women also find strength from closer sources of support.

While mom, daughter, sis or significant other is out on the course, Ironmates get to test their own endurance on the course. Playing spectator all day in the hot sun or spending a week at a triathlon venue around ultrafit tri-crazed athletes, isn't exactly everyone's idea of a fun holiday.

The dedicated Ironmate, however, knows that no pleasure cruise or tranquil beach can bring the same kind of enjoyment as being part of the celebration of human spirit that happens over 140.6 miles. By taking the time to involve others, you will also be able to leave a lasting impression on them that can change their lives for the better.

Consider the impact on the daughters of 2004 World Ironman age-group champion Kathy Winkler, who get to watch mom as a role model of success while she participates in the Ironman Hawaii. They also get to have fun while on their "triathlon vacation."

Winkler's youngest daughter, JoJo, said, "It is amazing how so many people are such great athletes and can do this amazing race. We did fun things before the race, like go snorkeling and hiking in the volcanoes, playing in the pool and ocean. My sister and I would kayak with my mom while she was in the lagoon. Sometimes we rode our bikes while she ran."

Winkler's other daughter, Mattie, added, "I like going to the very end of the race at midnight. You get to see a lot of people who do the race, but they don't put on TV because they aren't the winners. Sometimes they have a harder race, they are out there all day until midnight and it is fun to support them. I like to see how happy people are when they finish … I liked getting ice cream at the end, too!"

Mom Winkler, who placed 5th in 35-39 in 2005, has provided her daughters with the kind of trip souvenir that you can't get at a theme park – inspiration. "After watching and helping my mom go through all the preparations for Ironman, it makes me want to try it."

Rodger Bivens also knows what it is like to introduce a family member to triathlon and then play support role. As husband to Karin Bivens, who competed in the 60-64 age-group at her first Hawaii Ironman in 2005, his perspective as an age-grouper himself helped him to relate to what she was going through. "I knew the difficult training regimen she had been through and how exciting and unnerving race week is. However, what is especially tough about being a supporter is that you desperately want to be out there preparing for and doing the race yourself."

Karin Bivens, along with her husband Rodger, at the finish line of her first Ironman World Championships in 2005.

Bivens did his best to keep himself busy and support his wife with daily swims, morning runs and relaxation reminders. "In general, my job was to try and have Karin relax as much as possible and keep positive race thoughts in her mind, particularly when nervousness and doubt began creeping in."

His race-day support strategy included volunteering for three positions: swim to bike transition area; bike to run transition area; and finish line catcher, enabling him to see his wife through the transitions and, most importantly, watch her run down the brightly lit chute an hour and a half before the midnight cut-off.

"I was able to greet and congratulate her as she became a 'Hawaiian Ironman,'" Bivens said. "It was a great experience for both of us. And Karin has accomplished something that some of the rest of us are still striving for ... to be a Hawaiian Ironman."

California's Scott Silver also knows what its like to have a great Hawaii experience for both himself and his significant other, Kiki Rutowski, who placed 14th in the 30-34 age-group in 2005. He, too, raced and cheered Kiki along the way.

"It was fun to be out there with Kiki on race day," said Silver who finished Kona in 9:43 while keeping an eye out for his girlfriend. "I am always a little nervous until I see her on the bike. This year I didn't see her until the run, and I had all sorts of bad thoughts going through my head. Kiki is extremely focused on the run, but I was able to get a high five and ear-to-ear smile from her on Alii Drive, plus a 5-second summary of her bike ride and swim."

Still, Silver prefers doing the day together, rather than having Kiki on the sidelines cheering. "At Ironman Couer D'Alene this year, I had the opportunity to compete while Kiki was a spectator. While I enjoyed not having to worry about her race or safety, I didn't like the race being just about me. Since Kiki and I spend countless hours training together, the event is always enriched when we collectively 'toe the line' and share the experiences on the day."

Silver summarizes well the sentiments for many Ironmates around the globe. "It's always a challenge, but we will be back at it next year for sure."

Get into giving – It is proven that volunteering and charitable actions are good for our health and longevity. It's more than just physical fitness that gives us increased vitality. There are many opportunities out there to give back to the sport, but purpose for training can be greatly enhanced by participating in a charitable fundraising event or team.

The best-known include:
- **Team-in-Training,** which takes individual sports like running, cycling and triathlon, and enlists teams of people to train together and raise funds for the Leukemia and Lymphoma Society. (See www.teamintraining.org)
- **Komen Race for the Cure**, the largest series of 5k run/walks in the world has raised $453 million for breast cancer research, education and treatment. (See www.komen.org)
- **MS Bike Tour** has wheeled across the country to become the largest cycling event in America, raising $450 million for multiple sclerosis research along the way. It's two-day, 150-mile endurance treks aren't just for the hardcore. The Tour includes a wide range of rides, with 100 different tours in 49 states in the U.S. (See www.nationalmssociety.org)

Janus Charity Challenge is an innovative fundraising program that helps add more depth and meaning to an athlete's Ironman triathlon experience. The program is unique in that there is no designated beneficiary – participants can choose to raise funds for the charity he or she is most passionate about. To inspire athletes to participate, Janus, a U.S. investment management firm, makes additional contributions to the beneficiaries of the top fundraisers at each race. Since the program's inception in 2001, the Janus Charity Challenge has raised over $12 million for hundreds of deserving nonprofit organizations across the United States. (See www.januscharitychallenge.com)

World class giving tri women – Diana Hassel, Lydia Delis-Schlosser and Cherie Gruenfeld

Diana Hassel and Lydia Delis-Schlosser know what it is like to stand on the podium as the best women in the world of Ironman triathlon. Hassel was the 2002 Champion (30-34 age-group) and Delis-Schlosser was the 2004 Champion (45-49 age-group). No doubt endless hours of disciplined training juggled with their full-time jobs – Hassel in veterinary medicine in Colorado and Delis-Schlosser in architecture in California – brought them to this place. Delis-Schlosser also juggles parenting two teenage sons, so if her plate isn't full enough already, it is truly inspiring that both she and Hassel put extra effort toward goals bigger than just placing on the podium again at the 2005 World Ironman Championships in Hawaii.

Both put hard work into their quest to become charitable champs. Along with their triathlon racing efforts, they joined the Janus Charity Challenge to raise funds for their friend and fellow Ironwoman Sue Robinson who battled ovarian cancer in 2004.

Cherie Gruenfeld is another all-round champion Ironwoman. She has garnered the title of World Ironman age-group Champion six times so far and has held the world record for the women's 55-59 category, among other bests. And what's more – she's been on a Wheaties box!

Like Diana and Lydia, Cherie knows that it's worth striving for a deeper championship in the form of philanthropy. She founded a non-profit project to benefit disadvantaged, at-risk youth in California. Cherie also participated in the Janus Charity Challenge for Ironman Coeur D'Alene in 2005. She didn't come out tops on the donations, but exceeded her goal – not unexpected for a woman who calls her non-profit project Exceeding Expectations!

"Exceeding Expectations attempts to re-direct the lives of at-risk, inner-city kids in San Bernardino, California, using the sport of triathlon. To say that it has been a success would be a vast understatement!" said Cherie. "Despite overwhelming odds, the kids in the program have successfully avoided drifting off into the kind of life that a few years ago seemed all but inevitable. Their grades are up, their behavior in school has been exemplary, and one has become the first of the bunch – and the first in his family – to graduate from high school." (See www.leegruenfeld.com for more info on Exceeding Expectations.)

"Remarkably, he's starting college in the fall, which is something that wouldn't even have been considered a distant possibility a few years ago."

CHAPTER 8

Get a Coach

It is rare to see an Olympic athlete or professional sports team without a coach. If you are striving to do the best you can with the time and resources you have, then you will benefit from having a coach, no matter what your level of performance is.

A coach can guide you and prevent you from making time-consuming, frustrating mistakes or worse – injury and burnout. Women are typically good about seeking out help and expert guidance so it's usually a matter of how to find the right coach and how to develop a coach-athlete relationship that is beneficial for you.

There are good reasons to work with a qualified triathlon coach. Self-coached athletes often make unnecessary mistakes, such as not taking enough recovery time, training at inappropriate heart rates given the athlete's goals or background, skipping cross-training or strength sessions, racing too often, and failing to adequately prepare mentally or nutritionally, especially for long races.

According to Barrie Shepley, Canada's Triathlon Coach of the Year in 2005, "Research indicates that an athlete is unlikely to reach his or her full potential if they are training without the support and supervision of a qualified coach. I have seen hundreds of extremely talented athletes that never reached their potential because they lacked the direction, support and mentoring of a qualified coach."

Many athletes try to coach themselves, but even the best can benefit from an outside objective perspective. While it is important for an athlete to listen carefully to herself and her indicators to direct her training, it is very rare that an outside expert, even just a mentor, will not improve an athlete's chances of implementing their best plan. "Self-coached athletes generally fall into one of two groups," said Shepley. "Over-motivated or under-motivated. Over-motivated athletes believe that 'more is better' and while they make big improvements early in training development, they generally overtrain, become injured and ultimately burn out. Under-motivated athletes, on the other hand, might have phases of solid training but ultimately lack the discipline and consistency to achieve significant improvements."

Working with a coach paid off for Jennifer Johnson when she won her age-group at the 2006 Buffalo Springs Lake Triathlon.

Your best strategy

There are many training articles and books out there that provide generic triathlon training plans and, of course, these are much more financially attractive than a private, personal coach. However, the input of an experienced triathlete, trained coach or mentor will be worth a great deal in creating the individualized plan you need for your specific goals. An individualized plan will help you to maximize your personal strengths and overcome your weaknesses.

A coach can see your situation from an outside perspective, understand the path you are headed down, help you identify your limitations to meeting your goals, and assist you in developing a detailed road map to success that best employs your own skills and strengths. A coach or mentor will take care of devising your unique strategy, and you can focus on executing the plan.

It's the little things, too

A coach can help you develop more than just what to do in terms of swim, bike, run, but also the little things that, when added up, make a big difference to your success and enjoyment of the sport, and ultimately longevity in the sport. A supportive coach who helps you to make the most of your situation and to adapt to the challenges along the way will likely help you stay involved in the sport for the long run.

More than contributing to just the physical aspect of your training, a coach's input into your nutrition and mental plans, and your emotional and spiritual development, can make a huge difference.

A coach will ensure you are not missing out on those little things that add up over many seasons – nutrition guidance, body composition considerations, biomechanics and technique analysis, flexibility and core stability strength, race plans and reflection, and season-end reviews. A coach will help coordinate the small details into the big picture, keep you healthy physically and mentally, and growing year after year.

Keep it in perspective

If you are investing your valuable time into pursuing the sport, even at the recreational level, optimizing your time with a plan best for you will help you improve and also enjoy triathlon in a harmonious way that is well-integrated with the rest of your life.

For some, the sport can be all-consuming, but if you're looking for the balanced approach, a coach can be your greatest helper toward that aim.

A coach can also play the role of cheerleader and lift you back up when you experience inevitable obstacles and disappointments. Rarely does everything go according to plan, but a coach can help you dust yourself off and get back on the horse with the new direction you need.

For the impatient who might become disenchanted by a lack of quick results – a common ailment of our society in general – a coach can keep your progress in perspective and reassure you that you are making steps, however small and slow, toward your goals. Coaches can help athletes instill patience and a process-oriented mindset, which allows for a focus on the joy of the journey no matter the end results. And that joy is, after all, what women are striving for when they put on their swim caps and dive in to the unknown waters of their triathlon endeavors.

Trust and belief
When you engage in a coaching relationship, assuming you have found someone with the certification credentials and knowledge of the particular distance you are focused on, the two most important qualities to nurture are trust and belief – from both sides.

Trust in your coach's plan and your ability to execute it. It may be hard, but the intention of a coach is to help push you out of your comfort zones and into new territory. Communicating closely with your coach will allow you to keep pushing your boundaries, but have your coach prevent you from falling over.

If you are the highly motivated type, you will likely do best with a coach who pulls in the reigns and gets you to rest when you truly need to, rather than a slave-driver coach who is better for those with less motivation. As a coach myself for a number of highly motivated women, my job often becomes getting them to pull back before they injure themselves.

Belief in your coach's direction is critical. Similarly, the coach's belief in the athlete is fundamental to ensuring the relationship flourishes.

Finding the right fit
Dave Scott, six-time Ironman legend, said it best when he described the fickleness of the athlete-coach relationship in his October 2005 article for *Triathlete Magazine*. "A coach can be well trained and highly successful

but often, due to no one's fault, a coach/athlete relationship may not flourish. I've seen brilliant coaches that fully grasp the scientific applications of training but don't have the empathy or awareness to connect with particular athletes."

The number of triathlon coaches out there has grown exponentially. When looking for a coach consider the following:

1. Is the coach certified in triathlon? (USAT and other national governing bodies for triathlon have certification programs. USAT-certified coaches are listed on their web site.)
2. Does the coach have the education, knowledge and experience in triathlon and other aspects such as nutrition, strength training and psychology that you need?
3. Can the coach develop a periodized program for you that fits with your goals and lifestyle?
4. How many athletes is the coach already working with? What other commitments does the coach have that may impede his or her ability to provide you with attention?
5. What kind of success is she or he having with athletes? (testimonials or references recommended)
6. What kind of flexibility for changes is the coach capable of?
7. Can they offer objective advice in the best interest of the athlete?
8. Do they have the ability to observe technique at a detailed level in all three sports and suggest effective drills and focus for changes? Or can they refer you to an expert?
9. Are they available in person or will the relationship be by phone and emails?
10. Are they able to communicate effectively at your level?
11. Does their personality and coaching philosophy appeal to you?
12. Are the fees demanded in line with the services offered and their experience level?

Women coaches in triathlon

A good coach can coach either gender, however, some coaches have more success coaching a specific gender due to some of the subtle differences between men and women, especially in the novice ranks. Also, some women triathletes prefer a female coach, especially the beginners, since they feel more comfortable in a new, potentially unnerving, situation with the support of a fellow female. However, there are some women who respond better with a male coach, especially at the elite level when a more masculine-like competitive drive is key to success.

Thankfully, there are many female coaches in the sport of triathlon even at the highest level. In fact, Gale Bernhardt served as the USA Olympic Team coach in Athens and chairs the USAT Coaching Commission as the only female member. See www.galebernhardt.com for more information on Gale's consulting business.

USA Triathlon provides an online listing of all their certified coaches with contact information and specialty focus at www.usatriathlon.org under "Find a Coach."

At the beginner level, women coaches are very accessible, especially in cities where demand is driven by the large Danskin Women's Triathlon or other women-only events. The Women's Commission is a volunteer organization under USAT with the mandate to encourage women of all ages to participate in the sport and ensure equality, recognition and rewards for women in multisport. The Commission is also a resource for women coaches as it provides annual grants to women conducting clinics that help education and introduce women to triathlon.

See www.usatwomen.com to find a list of clinics and women coaches supporting women-specific training programs. The Resources section at the back of this book includes a partial list of women who belong to the Women's Commission and offer clinics or programs specifically for women.

The difference a coach makes – Jennifer Johnson's story

Until last year, I just showed up to races and hoped for the best. I had no focus, no training, no organization, no goals. In 2004, I did the Buffalo Springs Lake Triathlon (BSLT) and missed the slot to qualify for the World Ironman Championships by just 42 seconds! That gave me a taste of how hard it was to qualify. My goal in 2005 was to qualify. I went to coach Larry Krutka in February, told him that I wanted to qualify for Kona, and we went from there. He was a long time friend (father of my high school best friend), so I was fortunate to have an established relationship with him. He was also a five-time podium finisher at Kona!

I did Ralph's California Half-Ironman in March, and my time was 5:54 – obviously a long way from qualifying. I did BSLT again in June ... and totally bonked on the run ... did not qualify again. As a last-ditch effort, I went to Vineman and finished in a PR 4:53 for 3rd in my age-group, 7th overall, and qualified! Two weeks later, I went to the USAT Long Course National Championship and won the USAT 25-29 age-group national championship and placed 3rd overall in a time of 4:59. I am pretty excited that I knocked nearly an hour off of my half-IM time this season. Having a coach really helped to focus my training.

Larry is a very busy personal trainer and only coached me as a personal favor, so I switched to working with Kevin Purcell (www.coachkp.com). Kevin and I have been working closely together since October 2005. I was really fortunate to find him. I was worried about finding an "on-line" coach, but Kevin is anything but an "on-line" coach. We regularly talk on the phone and exchange emails, and he is absolutely wonderful. He has saved me from injury (and from overtraining/too much intensity), and I have dramatically improved in all three sports.

I think the key to a good coach is open communication ... questioning your coach, asking "why", getting feedback about workouts, etc. Through our communication, I have really come to trust Kevin, which is essential (in my opinion) to having success with a coach. You have to be honest with your coach — from clearly articulating your long-term goals to the day-to-day training issues. I tell Kevin when I am tired, when I am feeling twinges, potential injuries, when I am having other stressors in my life that impact my ability to train, etc. Kevin is very knowledgeable and has a true sense of balance.

I did Ralph's California Ironman 70.3 in March 2006 and it was my first race of the season. I had come down with a bad case of the flu in early February (2 entire weeks off). Not only was Kevin able to alter my training and still get me to the starting line, but I improved on my 2005 time by nearly 45 minutes, placed 7th in my age-group and 17th overall.

PART 4
Get Training

"Winning is accomplished in the preparation phase, not the execution phase." – Dr. Robert Anthony

The three chapters in Part Four will help you make smart training, nutrition and racing choices. Making these decisions requires plenty of preparation – gathering information, understanding your challenges and goals, and creating effective plans for specific triathlon situations.

Many women want to be told exactly what to do, what to eat, and what to include in their race plans. However, it is important to remember that we are **individuals**. The best plans for you are unique to you. The following chapters aim to help you understand and develop your own unique plans for training, nutrition and racing that are best for you and your situation.

CHAPTER 9
Training Plans

WHY TRAIN?

It is advised at this point that you quickly review Chapter 2: Preparing Your Mind with an assessment of your strengths and weaknesses and development of your goals.

An important question to ask at this point is – **Why are you training?**

Are you training to lose weight? Look better? Have more stamina and energy for your family? Improve your lifestyle? Improve your social life? Do you want to place in your age-group? Finish an Ironman? Qualify for the World Championships?

While outcomes and results are important, the more focused your motive to train is on the process, the more effective and beneficial your training is likely to be.

Ask yourself these questions: what do you care about that is lasting and genuinely healthy for you? Are you enjoying what you are doing? Does triathlon improve the quality of your life with your body, mind and spirit? Are you at your best?

If these are hard to answer, consider the bigger picture of your life. What will matter when you are nearing the end of your life? This is what the triathlon life is about: Lifelong rewards that go beyond a lower heart rate and slimmer waistline.

Texas triathlete Shorey Russell became more serious about triathlon last year and found benefits beyond fitness that helped her to answer the "Why."

"Getting more serious about triathlon this year has had tremendous benefits for me at work. I am more confident, outspoken, motivated, and have more initiative than ever," said the software specialist.

"Cheering me on at races has also had benefits for my family – my sisters are training, and my mom was even motivated to add physical exercise to her schedule. My parents are training for a half marathon.

That 'how to lose weight and have great abs' approach really makes me smile. I think a lot of women shortchange – or have a tendency to shortchange – themselves in that way of thinking. I have been practicing yoga for several years, and it's very similar. It's not about the workout, it's about the journey to achieve spiritual and emotional balance and really is life changing. As a supplement to my biking, swimming and running, it also gives me an excellent way to stretch, builds core strength, helps me keep my spirit up, and forces me to not take myself too seriously. All this is really important for a novice triathlete."

Doise Miers, also of Austin, Texas, shares her experience with triathlon training. "I know personally I have grown and am able to sort out the joys of life and enjoy them more. I'm not sure how this ties in athletically but I know my friends who don't get outside and exercise just don't enjoy the small things like I do. The average woman who works, maybe has kids and family obligations which limit her time – I think these women get turned off exercise and being healthy in general because they take an 'all or nothing' approach and many things or programs seem too overwhelming.

"Having accomplished something that most people can't even imagine (Doise has run several 50-80K ultra races) gives you more confidence which, sadly, many women currently lack. I have been empowered as an individual through athletics, and I have been able to pass that on to other family members and friends. I'm more secure with myself and know that this makes a difference in relationships with people, not just the personal ones, but those at the workplace and just being out in the world in general. And, of course, there's the constant amazement of what I, as not-a-particularly athletic person, have accomplished."

Take a moment to consider why you tri and write down some of the benefits you may not have thought of before. Ask others close to you in your family or workplace if they have noticed any benefits to your life, or even theirs. Remember these as motivation for your next triathlon.

THE BEST PLAN FOR YOU

When devising a plan, it is most important to consider your starting level of fitness, your training experience and whether the plan will be balanced in terms of frequency with each of the sports or focused on a higher frequency in a particular sport in order to make specific improvements.

The most important characteristic for long-term success is consistency and repeated practice. Because consistency and practice are of utmost importance, avoidance of injury must be a high priority. Long breaks due to injury are detrimental. Thus, a balanced program with appropriate volumes and session intensity are important, as well as good biomechanical form, to promote efficient injury-free development. A key benefit of triathlon is that it allows cross-training to distribute the training stress around to different body parts through the different activities, so often triathletes can handle higher volumes than one-sport athletes.

It is not unexpected then that the number of annual hours for elite athletes is dramatically higher than age-groupers and more recreational beginners. The typical annual hours for elites is 800-1100; top age-groupers, 500-1000; average age-groupers, 300-600; and beginners, 200-300.

The number of weekly hours to plan will depend on your experience and base, your time point in the season, the event you are training for, and your recovery ability due to outside stressors.

Minimal suggested required training for each distance

Distance	Weekly hours	Minimal weeks expected	Your plan
Sprint	3-6	6	
Olympic	6-10	8	
Half or 70.3	10-14	10-16	
Full ironman distance	14-20	12-16	

Once you know the time frame you wish to plan for (most often called an Annual Training Plan or ATP), with a priority event to peak for, the progression throughout the season can be developed with cycles or blocks of training interspersed with recovery periods. This is known as periodization and will be discussed in more detail below later.

Consulting with an experienced coach is the best way to assess your situation and goals. A coach will be able to help you strategize for your season based on various inputs, such as starting fitness, technical limitations, time available weekly, and specific race plans.

CREATING BALANCED TRAINING PROGRAMS

A balanced program will incorporate:
1. Your short and long term goals
2. The F.I.T.T. (Frequency, Intensity, Time, Type) equation with each variable appropriately added so your system is not overloaded
3. Different phases with a Base Foundation and Pyramid Build, and Peak (see diagram on page 138)
4. Recovery cycles

Basic training program factors
F.I.T.T. = FREQUENCY. INTENSITY. TIME. TYPE

F.I.T.T.ness programs can be made simple by considering when and how to apply these four variables to your own plan. Variables to consider in the formula are based on your stage of development, your goals, and your strengths and weaknesses.

Frequency – refers to the number of times you do a particular activity
Intensity – refers to how hard or easy you do the activity with respect to your HR training zones
Time – refers to the duration that you do an activity
Type – the kind of activity, which has the potential to add more or less stress to the body, i.e., running versus swimming

Consider that each person begins with a F.I.T.T. equation of a certain capacity. By adding stress to one side of the equation, your system's capacity can grow so long as the variables are effectively added and do not overstress the system. If you go overboard with too much duration or intensity before your body and mind are ready for it, it will lead to possible burnout or injury and less effective recovery and progress.

PERIODIZATION OF YOUR PROGRAM

Principles:
- Divide the year into phases
- Peak for events by progression work and skill development in each phase
- General to specific
- Unique to athlete needs
- Structure provides focus training, rest and recovery
- Annual plan (macrocycle), phase (mesocycle), week (microcycle)
- Prioritize events as "A" most important, "B" important, "C" train through

A. ESTABLISH SEASON PHASES

Pre/post-season – rest, rejuvenate body and mind, enjoy low-intensity aerobic activities

Early Base Phase – skills focus on efficiency, aerobic endurance (low intensity), building in order of frequency, duration, load (intensity)

Late Base Phase – skills focus continues, introduce muscular endurance (low intensity with more hills/resistance), strength training

Build Phase – maintain endurance and continue to build strength, more frequency and duration in this phase

Peak Phase – Reduce time and frequency variables, increase intensity and duration of intervals

Taper Phase – Active recovery, low intensity mixed with short high intensity intervals

The Event!

A periodized plan starts with a base foundation and builds with more strength peaks with more speed

Peak – Speed, specific strength, intervals

Build – Strength, muscular endurance, resistance, force

Base – Foundation, freq, skills, aerobic endurance, core structure

B. SEASON GOALS/EVENTS IDENTIFIED – Identify your priority A race, B events, and C events on the calendar and work the rest of the phases to build to an A race. Consider peaking for two, at most, three key A races, especially if you are doing long-distance events. That will allow you to really maximize your potential and hopefully experience breakthrough races after you have given your body the appropriate taper period and recovery.

C. TRAINING OBJECTIVES – Identify the smaller steps needed to address weaknesses or limitations and to focus training efforts for effective improvement. Each workout should reflect one of the set training objectives, which in turn prepares for the season goal above. Look over the Chapter 2 strengths and weaknesses you wrote down and consider which areas you wish to work on in order to provide yourself the most effective results toward achieving your goals. If a poor open water swim has been leaving you behind, for example, consider adding in a weekly open water swim, practicing swim to bike bricks (see p. 140) and training in a group situation to simulate open water racing. Write down your training objectives in the list on top of your training calendar. Consider one of your objectives to be "to have fun!"

D. THE ATP (ANNUAL TRAINING PLAN)

Ironman Training Program Example

Phase	Duration	Type		Intensity	Time/Freq	Event
		Endurance	Strength	(% of max heart rate)	(low hours recovery)	
Early Base	10 weeks	Swim, run	Endur. weights 12-15 reps	Low ‹70%	6-10 hours	10 k run
Late Base	9 weeks	Run, swim	Endur. Wts 12-15 reps Hills run	Low ‹70%	8-12 hours	30 k run
Build	13 weeks	Bike, run, swim, bricks	Stren. Wts 10 reps Power Wts 6-8 reps	Low –med 70-85%	8-16 hours	Triathlon
Peak	3 weeks	Bike, run, bricks, swim	Maint. Wts 8-12 reps 1x/week	Low -high	8-12 hours	Half Ironman
Taper	3 weeks		Maint. Wts	Low recovery	8-10 hours	Rest

E. WEEKLY PLANNING

Consider the following factors when developing each week's plan:
1. Time limitations – work and family schedule, meetings, vacations, social life – remember the importance of striking a BALANCE and integrating triathlon harmoniously with the rest of your life.

2. Establish key workouts – These are the critical sessions or breakthrough workouts that will bring you to a new level of fitness or are key steps to achieve goals. These are the must-do workouts, such as the long run in marathon training or long brick for an Ironman. Make it a priority appointment with yourself.

3. Establish key workout placement – Scheduling the optimal days for these key sessions is the next important planning step. Consider two-sport brick (swim-bike or bike-run) sessions to get the most of your training time.

4. Recovery – Once the key workout(s) has been put on the week's calendar, plan to rest following stressful workouts.

5. Remaining workouts inserted are based on the phase (i.e., in the base phase add more frequency, aerobic sessions with form emphasis) and your strengths/weaknesses.

6. Include periodic testing – Consider including monthly testing of your aerobic endurance and lactate levels to make sure your training is moving in the right direction. Consult a guide, such as *The Triathlete's Training Bible* by Joe Friel, for specifics on testing.

7. Rescheduling – As can happen to anyone, things don't always go according to plan and things need adjusting. Focus on staying on task and do the best to re-plan key workouts. Avoid the trap of trying to make up missed workouts too often.

Examples:

Key workouts –

1. Endurance – year round

2. Strength – early phases (these workouts include weights and core in the gym and hill/force training on the bike or run)

3. Lactate threshold – build, peak phases

4. Speed intervals – peak phase (not more than 5-15% of total weekly hours, depending on distance training with lower percentage of interval training done with Ironman training)

5. Recovery – year round (active recovery sessions are very low intensity workouts)

6. Skills – year round (for these workouts, use the sport skills guidance provided in Chapter 5)

7. Brick – build, peak phases (brick workouts involve doing two sports back-to-back with little or no rest, such as swim-to-bike, or bike-to-run)

Workout Examples in Phases:

Base: swim technique, cycling endurance, running endurance, core strength, intensity at 70% max heart rate

Build: swim muscular endurance (i.e., add pull and paddle sets), running and cycling hills, continuous tempo runs or cycling for 20-60 minutes, power intervals on bike (30 seconds max output with five-minutes rest), strength core or weight training (at an intensity 70-80% max heart rate depending on session)

Peak: long intensive intervals (3-8 minute at or just below lactate threshold heart rate), power weights (6-8 reps), long day race simulations

Taper: intense intervals (race pace) 2-5 minutes at or above lactate threshold, recovery

ANNUAL TRAINING PLAN SAMPLE CALENDAR

FOCUS GOAL EVENT: _____

Training Objectives 1.

2.

3.

4.

Phase/ Week	M	T	W	TH	F	S	Su

Additional resources to create training plans

As you attempt to develop a training program best for you, consider consulting with a qualified coach or using one of Gale Bernhardt's books for self coached athletes.

Training Plans for Multisport Athletes, by Gale Bernhardt is a book containing fourteen detailed training plans for triathlon, duathlon and X-Terra events. There are plans for sprint triathlons, Olympic triathlons, half-Ironman distance triathlons and Ironman-distance triathlons. This great training resource contains three-month, six-month and year-long plans.

Triathlon Training Basics, by Gale Bernhardt is a book that contains four detailed training plans to help first-time triathletes prepare for a sprint triathlon or an Olympic distance triathlon. Two plans are designed for already-fit beginners and two plans are for currently unfit beginners. There are also four plans per sport (swimming, cycling and running) for individuals wanting to train for a triathlon as a single-sport team member. The plans can be used in succession, helping you progress from a triathlon team member to a triathlete. The book contains strength training, stretching and bike fit photos to help you get started on the right track.

Workouts in a Binder® is another product co-authored by Bernhardt with swim workouts for triathletes. These handy workout cards help athletes and coaches optimize workouts and are waterproof to prevent damage from water, sweat and dirt.

SIGNS OF OVERTRAINING OR UNDERRECOVERY

If you have increased your variables of your F.I.T.T. equation too fast or too soon, you may experience signs of overreaching (which is easy to overcome with a day or two of lighter training or rest) or worse, overtraining, which may need more time to recover from. Some athletes may push themselves so far that they are no longer able to do effective workouts and must take several weeks or even months to return to a state of health.

Indicators that you may be fatigued from training or other stressors in your life include:

- High heart rate upon waking (the easiest monitor)
- Heart rate lower in training and a struggle to increase despite increasing effort
- Sleep disturbance
- Appetite changes
- Irritable mood

TRAINING LOGS

It is highly recommended that you keep a record of the training you have completed. When a cumulative record is developed, patterns are more visible from week to week, month to month and year to year. This can help and guide you in future workouts and yearly planning. You may have seasonal rhythms that become more evident by keeping an accurate log. For instance, you may see what months or seasons are best for focused training or rejuvenation periods. It may also help you focus on the little victories and results in each workout or week that may not be so obvious in racing results, such as hitting a certain frequency of swim workouts, volume of bike hours, or mile repeats at a certain pace on the track.

Your training log should record frequency of each sport and duration, total aerobic hours and total training hours, including strength and stretching time. Also, very beneficial to include are sleep hours, stress levels, muscle soreness and fatigue levels. Like a diary, other qualitative notes can be added, such as feelings of joy related to breakthroughs. It also keeps you accountable and honest. People often think they are doing a certain amount of training, but without a written record, their perceptions may be off. There is no hiding once you have it as permanent record.

When you start, changes and improvements are quickly visible, which keep you motivated. As you progress and hit more plateaus, more training is required to receive smaller increments of improvement. It may help if you decrease your volume or intensity at times in order to avoid reoccurrences of fatigue or overtraining. It helps you to become more aware of your body as you record and potentially see signals of sickness, injury or overtraining coming on.

Training logs can be done in a written book such as Sally Edwards' *Triathlon Log* or Joe Friel's *Inside Triathlon Training Diary: A Weekly Log for Tracking Your Multisport Fitness,* a spiral-bound book. Hand written diaries are good for subjective records, however, a digital format, such as spreadsheet or online software program, can allow for additional objective and systematic analysis, including such useful features as tracking mileage of wear on a particular pair of shoes. A number of online logs can be found at no cost or have a small fee.

Online logs:
- Trainingpeaks.com
- BeginnerTriathlete.com
- Dailytrain.com
- Ontri.com
- Trifuel.com

CHAPTER 10
Nutrition

YOU ARE WHAT YOU EAT

It is a common cliché, however, it is true. Every three to six months, our body regenerates every cell from the building blocks provided in our nutrient intakes. You are a product of the choices you make.

Food is also fuel. Fueling our body with what it needs allows us to endure the activities we demand from it, and supports our vitality and state of health.

Many women want some quick fix or to be told to eat particular foods. I believe everyone is unique in this regard, and what you need to find – and learn for yourself – is what is best for you. Call it your nutritional intelligence. World champion triathlete Siri Lindley calls it "being tuned in" to her body's needs. While there are fundamentals to understand, consider how to adapt your nutrition to your own situation. We are all entirely unique. We are also dynamic beings so we are always changing, and with that, our needs are subtly changing. The key is to stay in tune with what our needs are.

The shelves are flooded with books on the subject of nutrition. The following books on my shelf have weighed heavily in helping me better understand the building blocks of nutrition and adapt my nutrition strategies for healthy living, improved body composition, and better training and racing.

- *Sports Nutrition for Endurance Athletes* by Monique Ryan
- *The Paleo Diet* by Loren Cordain
- *Going Long* by Joe Friel and Gordo Byrn
- *Optimum Sports Nutrition* by Dr. Michael Colgan
- *The Path to Phenomenal Health* by Sam Graci
- *The Performance Zone* by John Ivy and Robert Portman

Other books to consider as good resources include Nancy Clark's *Sports Nutrition Guidebook* and *Eating Well for Optimum Health* by Andrew Weil.

NUTRITION INTELLIGENCE

From my own experience and research, I believe nutrition has a huge impact on our well-being, athletic training, improvement and performances. Many athletes do not give nutrition its due credit, and as a result they struggle more than they need to.

In 2002, I did a nutrition overhaul and could feel the tremendous difference it makes, especially with recovery. It is still an ongoing self-discovery to be nutritionally intelligent and self-aware to what my body truly needs. It took an injury that prevented me from training aerobically to see how I had used working out as a cover up for my poor nutrition habits.

While I think that it is important that you don't deny yourselves of food, I think that those of you looking for body composition changes and healthier lives, it is important you stay conscious of what you are nurturing your body with and when. Before you get frustrated with the scale not showing you numbers you'd like, be honest with yourself and become fully aware. Overlooking small decisions and choices to "slack" adds up and you can lose touch with what is optimal for the long-term health of your mind, body and spirit.

For women in particular, focusing on losing weight instead of improving nutrition is a common roadblock. Patience is also needed to stick to the new habits long enough to allow for the true transformations to take place. Small steps may be slow or frustrating, but they **will** get you there.

It is about the process – better nutrition **habits** incorporated into your long-term lifestyle and sustained by daily practice. Think about focusing on the process and body composition improvements, not weight. Avoid the scale. Also remember women tend to pay a much bigger price than men with their body composition due to non-adherence to nutritional excellence. Small positive habits make a difference. You are the product of thousands of tiny decisions.

Body composition
A woman has a different body composition than a man due to her differing biological function relating to childbirth. For women, the average amount of essential fat (for normal body function) is 12% of bodyweight and for men it is 3%, while storage fat (that which is deposited under the skin and also called subcutaneous fat) for men and women is fairly similar. A certain amount of body fat is vital for the body to function normally and healthily. In fact, striving for a body fat percentage that is too low can be dangerous and hinder recovery after hard training.

However, excess body fat is related to injury, non-adherence to training and overall reduced athletic performance. An excess of body fat acts as "dead weight," reducing speed and efficiency of movement.

World Champion Siri Lindley on Nutritional Intelligence

As an elite athlete, I have learned just how important the nutritional aspect is to your training, recovery and performance. Throughout my years of training, I have become so in tune to my body's needs that I am able to get the utmost out of my body each and every day. Everybody is different, and everybody needs to find the formula that works best for them, but this was mine:

- Never deprive your body. Your body works so hard for you every single day, it is absolutely crucial that you give it, in return, all those things it needs and that means feeding it the right foods, drinking plenty of water and satisfying cravings that are obviously signifying deficiencies. For example, I have been on some long rides where I start craving a steak, very strange indeed, but needs to be taken seriously as it means I need a bit of protein. Of course, if I am craving that carrot cake I saw in the bakery window that morning, that may be different, but if you are craving things like milk or meat, it usually means you are lacking something important.

- Drink plenty of water, all day. It really helps your body to function well.

- Allow yourself goodies. A little chocolate here or there does not hurt when you are training hard.

- Get plenty of protein, veggies, and fruits in your diet, preferably at every meal!

- Nuts and avocadoes, normally seen as no-nos, are actually great sources of good fat. Nuts are a great source of protein. Both are good energy sources, as well.

- My carbohydrate intake is mostly from the morning, after I wake up, until lunchtime. For dinner, I try to keep refined carbs, like potatoes, pasta and bread out, as you don't need it so much at night. It is a great way to keep your weight down.

Optimal body weight and composition for health and competition should be individual because of many factors – age, sex, genetics, and sport.

The American Council of Exercise provides the following General Body Fat Percentage Categories

Classification	Women (% fat)	Men (% fat)
Essential Fat	10-12%	2-4%
Athletes	14-20%	6-13%
Fitness	21-24%	14-17%
Acceptable	25-31%	18-25%
Obese	32% plus	25% plus

Body composition tests can be done via various methods, such as skin calipers or bioelectric impedance. However, a DEXA scan is the most accurate (and easy) and can provide a breakdown of fat-free mass and fat mass in the legs, arms and torso. This body composition information, when checked over a period of nutritional change and training, will allow you to assess how your nutrition and training programs are impacting your body composition. For instance, if you are losing muscle in your legs, along with fat, your program may benefit from more leg specific strength training.

The DEXA will help with those women who are very close to ideal body composition already and who struggle to drop pounds on the scale. During a year-long period of intensive nutrition focus, my weight stayed the same at 125-126 lbs; however, I started at 12% fat. At the next test, I was down to 10.2% fat, but I had added 3 lbs of muscle. In the final test, I was 7.9% fat, but had added 5 lbs of muscle, most of it in my legs due to training many miles of biking and running. Without the body composition check-ups, I would have been frustrated with the scale and cut back on calories, which would have hindered my training and ability to add lean muscle tissue. This is a major issue for many women who err by holding back on appropriate calories when training a lot.

COMMON MISTAKES WOMEN MAKE:
1. Eating too many sports bars
2. Eating processed foods, especially with high fructose corn syrup
3. Not eating enough lean protein
4. Not eating frequently enough (every 3-4 hours is optimal)
5. Not eating breakfast, especially before a workout (breakfast is for champions)
6. Consuming alcohol, then losing discipline by going extra on the portions and sweets

GUIDELINES FOR OPTIMAL NUTRITION

1. Consider food macronutrients (carbohydrates, fat, protein) as fuel sources essential for your body's maintenance of lean tissue, immune and reproductive functions and optimal athletic performance. With limited energy intake, the body will use fat and lean tissue for fuel. Loss of muscle results in the loss of strength and endurance. Inadequate energy intake relative to energy expenditure compromises performance and benefits associated with training. Eat to win!
2. Get the majority of energy from fruits, vegetables, and lean protein.
3. Eliminate processed foods.
4. Eat fresh whole carbohydrates from fruits and vegetables. Avoid refined white grains, starchy tubers and refined sugars, except when necessary for energy replenishment during and after long duration training sessions.
5. Include protein in every meal.
6. Never skip a meal.
8. Eat moderate fat with more good fats (monounsaturated and polyunsaturated) than bad (saturated) fats and near equal omega-3 and omega-6 fats.

MACRONUTRIENTS

Carbohydrate = 4 cal/g
Fat = 9 cal/g
Protein = 4 cal/g

Daily percentages of macronutrients – Depending on your nutritional strategy and your energy needs, your percentage for each macronutrient will vary. Typical healthy percentages are: carb 40-70%, protein 15-30%, fat 25-30%.

Carbohydrates – Carbohydrates maintain blood glucose during exercise and replace muscle glycogen. Recommended intake is 6 to 11 g/kg of body weight a day. Daily energy expenditure, sport, sex and environmental conditions factor into carbohydrate requirements.

Your daily CARBOHYDRATE range at 6-11g/kg of body weight: _____(g)

Fat – Fat intake (good sources) should not be restricted because there is no performance benefit in consuming a diet that is less than 15% energy from fat. Fat provides energy, fat-soluble vitamins and essential fatty acids. It requires glucose for metabolism.

Your daily FAT range at 20-25% of energy intake (total calories): _____(cal)

Protein – Protein requirements increase with activity. Endurance athletes need 1.2-1.4g/kg of body weight a day. Essential amino acids support cell structure, repair and maintain muscle and other body tissues, and are used for metabolism and endocrine and immune functions. Illness and injury can often be prevented by a steady protein intake. Protein is needed for the formation of hemoglobin, the oxygen-carrying portion of the blood. Consumption helps prevent iron-deficiency, or anemia. Foods with protein are also good sources of iron, zinc (needed for muscle growth and repair), and B vitamins.

Your daily PROTEIN range at 1.2-1.4g/kg of body weight: _____(g)

Not all protein sources are equal. Some top protein choices:
• Lean, hormone-free beef: High in iron, and one of the greatest sources of zinc, and B vitamins. Leaner cuts include: top round, eye of round, round tip. Look for beef that is greater than 90% (preferably 95%) lean. Beware that the percentage that is labeled on the packages is measured by weight and not by calories. For

example, "80% lean ground beef" is 80% lean by weight, but over 50% of its calories are from saturated fat.

- Lean, free-range chicken: Have been fed grains that are higher in omega. Stay away from eating the skin, which is high in fat and cholesterol.
- Eggs: High in cholesterol, yet great sources of omega-3 fatty acids. Especially healthful if they are from free-range chickens whose diet has been supplemented with an omega-3-rich diet.
- Fish: Many are great sources of omega-3 fatty acids, with salmon being the best. Lower in saturated fat than other animal protein sources. Farmed fish are usually less-desirable than wild because they are fed antibiotics and contain fewer omega-3 fatty acids due to low-nutritional value feed.
- Soy and other plant sources: Soy protein, edamame (fresh or frozen soybeans), some seeds (sesame, sunflower) and nuts (almonds, walnuts, hazelnuts), textured vegetable protein, tempeh. Plant sources of protein contain fiber and other micronutrients that animal sources lack and contain healthier fat sources. Therefore, it is a good idea to substitute some plant protein for animal sources. Be adventurous when trying soy products, but check labels to make sure they are not high in fat or contain unhealthful ingredients or additives. Try Boca burgers or garden burgers on a spelt bun with soy cheese for a real treat!
- Beans: Look for vegetarian refried, garbanzo beans, and kidney beans. Try hummus, a chickpea, sesameseed paste spread.
- Protein powder: Can be used in smoothies and hot cereals, and some may be used in baking breads and muffins. Different flavors can taste great!

MICRONUTRIENTS

Water – Makes up 70% of your body mass. Find more fluid recommendations later in this chapter.

Vitamins and minerals – Vitamins and minerals play an important role in energy production, hemoglobin synthesis, bone health, immune function, oxidative protection, and repairing muscle tissue. Minerals such as iron, zinc, selenium, and calcium are often low in female athletes with low/no animal product intake.

Water and electrolyte balance is also important for athletes. Gastric emptying is maximized when the amount of fluid in the stomach is high and reduced with hypertonic fluids or when carb concentration is greater than or equal to 8%. For that reason, sport drinks or special electrolyte solutions or tabs, such as Nuun, are beneficial for proper hydration. Sodium also helps the rehydration process by maintaining plasma osmolality and thus prompting the desire to drink.

NUTRITION CHECKLIST

Use a nutrition log for at least a week to assess how you are doing with some of these keys to good daily nutrition.

- Avoid refined sugars and processed foods.
- Meets recommended intake of protein, carbohydrate and fat (input your specific calculations)
  Protein: 1.2-1.4g/kg body weight, or _____ servings
  Carbs: 6-11 g/kg body weight, or _____ servings
  Fat: 20-25% of total calories, or _____ grams
- Balances carbohydrate, protein and fat at each meal.
- Drinks sufficient water with each meal and throughout the day.
- Eats at least 3-4 servings of fruit daily
- Eats at least 4-5 vegetable servings daily.
- Calcium intake: 1000-1500 mg calcium daily (2-3 dairy servings, if you eat dairy).
- Chooses a wide variety of colorful foods at each meal to maximize nutrient variety.
- Chooses fresh, wholesome, unprocessed foods (less sugar, salt and preservatives).
- Consistent eating with small snacks without going more than 4 hours not eating.
- Meets dietary fiber requirements (25-35 grams).
- Eats unsaturated fats in place of saturated when possible. Focuses on omega-3 fatty acid intake.
- Eats less cholesterol (less than 300 mg/day).
- Eats less sugar (less than 1 serving daily).
- Limits caffeine (less than 1-2 drinks/day).
- Eats slowly, in a relaxed environment, chewing food slowly.

EATING BEFORE, DURING AND AFTER TRAINING
(from "Nutrition" and "Athletic Performance" article, by The Position of Dietitians of Canada, the American Dietetic Association and the American College of Sport Medicine)

- The energy balance of normal, active people ranges from 37-41kcal/kg body weight a day. (Note that most triathletes with high-volume training regimens will require more calories than this.)
- Dehydration decreases performance. Athletes should drink 400-600ml two hours before exercise and 150-350ml every 15-20min. After exercise, fluid should be replaced.
- The before-exercise meal should provide sufficient fluid to maintain hydration, be relatively low in fat and fiber and relatively high in carbs, moderate in protein and composed of food well tolerated by athletes.
- During exercise, goals for nutrient consumption are to replace lost fluid and provide carbohydrates (30-60g/hr) for maintaining blood glucose levels. This is especially important for endurance training or racing more than an hour, when an athlete has not consumed adequate food before exercise, or in an extreme environment.
- After exercise, the dietary goal is to provide energy and carbs to replace muscle glycogen and ensure rapid recovery. Aim for a carb intake approximately 1-1.5g/kg body weight during the first 30 minutes and again every two hours for four to six hours to replace glycogen stores. Include protein as well to restore amino acids and repair muscle tissue.

Your post workout carbohydrate intake: _____

Types of foods and carb content:

Apple	20 g	Granola	18 g
Banana	25 g	Baked potato	55 g
Orange	20 g	Lentils (1 c)	40 g
Raisins (¼ c)	30 g	Beer (12 oz)	13 g
Carrot (1 med)	10 g	Soft drink (12 oz)	40 g
Bagel	30 g		

Nutrition resources on the web

For an easy way to keep track of your nutrition and the breakdown of macronutrients, consider using an online log like www.fitday.com or www.nutridiary.com. Another great web site for weight loss/maintenance support and information is www.cyberdiet.com.

Other web sites:
www.nalusda.gov/fnic/index.html (USDA government web site)
www.gssiweb.com (Gatorade Sport Science web site)
www.allrecipes.com (a great recipe and meal planning web site, with downloadable software for all aspects of your nutrition program, including some vegetarian recipes)
www.eatright.org (The American Dietetic Association web site)
www.glycemicindex.com (source to look up glycemic index for just about any food)
www.drweill.com
www.nancyclarkrd.com

www.nutribase.com (Professional Nutrition Software)
www.dietsoftware.com (Consumer Nutrition Software)
www.nbez.info (Nutrition Software for Novices)

PRE- AND POST-WORKOUT SMOOTHIE AND BAR RECIPES

Since pre- and post-workout nutrition is so important, here are a few recipe ideas shared by fellow triathlon women.

* C. = cup
T. = tablespoon
t. = teaspoon

Shorey's Pre-race Oatmeal Power Mix (Thanks to Shorey Russell, Austin, Texas)

Through trial and error, I have found the following recipe to be a great pre-race or long training day breakfast:
1/2 C. (or a single-serving package) instant oatmeal, plain
1 T. peanut butter
1 t. flax seed
1 t. honey
Handful of berries (blueberries, raspberries, strawberries, whatever)

Few slices of banana
Splash of water, enough to cover the oatmeal

Microwave on high for 1 minute. Then stir in 1 scoop of whey protein powder. (Note: If you put the protein powder in prior to cooking, it gets "hard").

I use only all-natural products, and this recipe includes items you can find all-natural in any grocery store. I have also changed it up and thrown in whatever fruit I happen to have in the kitchen – apples, peaches, figs, etc. It's easy enough to prepare when staying in a hotel for out-of-town races. I just freeze the fruit and then use hot water from the coffee maker to prepare it.

Natural Protein bars (Thanks to Gwen McLennan, Victoria, Canada)
Ingredients can be varied in proportion depending on how you like the consistency: Oats, protein powder, ground flax seeds, pumpkin seeds, sunflower seeds, peppermint extract, vanilla, cinnamon, milk or soy milk (enough to keep from being dry), peanut butter and coconut optional. Cook at 350° for about 8-10 minutes then cool and refrigerate.

Hillerie's Healthy Energy Bars (Thanks to Hillerie Denning, Victoria, Canada)
Preheat oven at 325° F
3 C. quick oats
1 C. dark chocolate chips
1 C. roasted sunflower seeds
1 C. sliced almonds
1 C. raisins or cranraisins or 1/2 C of each
1/2 C. melted butter
1 C. condensed milk
Mix all dry ingredients. Add melted butter. Bake in greased 9x 13 Pyrex pan.

Mylene's Smoothie (Thanks to Mylene Unterman, Austin, Texas)
1 C. soy milk (plain or vanilla)
1 C. yogurt (plain or flavored)
1 frozen banana
1 other fruit, i.e., handful of blueberries

Handful of ice cubes
Sometimes I will add 2 oz of tofu for extra protein
Blend really well (we have a Vita Mix blender, and it rocks!)

Lisa's Smoothies
Ingredients to add straight to blender:
Juices – i.e. orange, pineapple, etc
Unsweetened soy milk
Frozen berries or frozen fruits – i.e. blueberries, raspberries, blackberries, strawberries, peaches, cranberries, apples, melons, cherries, etc, or
Fresh fruits – i.e. bananas
Scoop of protein powder (various flavors to choose from such as vanilla or chocolate)
Depending on your calorie needs add in organic flax seed oil. (Especially good if your breakfast is low on fat)

Amy's Smoothie
Blend the following:
8 oz plain soy milk
1 scoop (approx. 2 T.) soy protein powder
1 frozen banana (freeze in foil)
1/2 cup frozen berries (buy them frozen)
2 T. flax meal (grind flax seeds in coffee grinder)
1 T. oat bran
Vitamin C powder

Makes a great breakfast or higher calorie snack-on-the-go!

Tara Smoothies (Thanks to Tara Ross www.taraross.ca, Victoria, Canada)
#1 – Quick 2 Recover + Energy 4 work day Smoothie
1 C. vanilla soy milk or chocolate *
1/2 C. raspberry yogurt (option to not include yogurt, and add and extra 1/2 C. of soy milk)
1 small frozen banana
1/2 C. frozen raspberries (or berry medley)
1 T. natural peanut butter ***

2 scoops of protein powder **
(If too thick, add 1/2 C. water or orange juice)

Mix in blender and bottoms up!

#2 – Awful Antioxidant Not-So-Smooth Smoothie (doesn't taste that great, but really gets rid of those free radicals after a hard intense training session)
1 C. vanilla soy milk *
1/2 C. blueberry yogurt
1 t. of spirulina (powder form)
1 small frozen banana
1 handful of almonds or walnuts****
2 scoops of protein powder **
If too thick, add 1/2 C. orange juice (or one t. frozen juice concentrate).

Blend away! This one may be a bit crunchier.

* Many flavored soy milks (vanilla, chocolate, etc.) are very high in sugar additives. A healthier option is to use plain, unsweetened soy milk and add a full teaspoon of honey – a natural sugar.
** Try to use organic fruits and protein powders (I personally use Hemp protein powder, although, it has a bit of a "grainy" taste) as there are less additives and sprays.
*** Instead of peanut butter, try other nut butters (such as cashew, hazelnut almond, walnut).
****Almonds and walnuts are also alkalinizing foods, so if you don't mind a "chewy" smoothie, use a handful of nuts instead of the nut butter, as nut butters tend to be a bit more expensive.

Mark's Marvelous Bars
2 bananas, mashed
2 egg whites
2 C. oats
1 t. vanilla
2 T. peanut butter
1/4 C. cranberries
1/4 C. pecans
1/4 C. coconut

Spray a 9 x 12 baking dish with cooking spray and preheat the oven to 325 degrees. In a bowl, mash bananas and blend with the egg whites, peanut butter and vanilla until blended. Then stir in oats, cranberries and pecans. Pour into baking dish and bake until done about 25 minutes.

Audrey van Eerden's Menopause Loaf (Thanks to Audrey van Eerden of Victoria, BC)
2 C. soy flour
2 C. brown whole wheat flour
2 C. rolled oats
1 C. slivered almonds
1 C. sunflower seeds
1 C. pumpkin seeds
1 C. ground flax seeds
2 T. malt extract or 2 T brown rice syrup
4 2/3 C. soy milk
1 t. ginger, all spice, and mace
3 C. raisins
3 pieces of candied ginger
2 greased loaf pans
Bake at 350° for 1 hour. Freeze sliced in zip lock bags.

Shae's Apple Sauce (Thanks to Shalane Carlson)
7-10 apples (best straight off a tree ... or free from a race!)
1/2 C. fresh pressed apple juice
1/2 C. pitted dates (for sweetness)
cinnamon to taste
cloves to taste

Peel and slice apples. Puree dates with 2 tbsp of apple juice. In a large pot at a very low heat, simmer apple chunks, remaining apple juice, date mixture, and spices. For extra nutritional value, puree apple peels and add near the end of the cooking process. Stir frequently, until apples are soft and broken up.

CHAPTER 11
Race ready

"Failure is not the inability to succeed. Rather, the unwillingness to put forth the effort." – Author unknown

There are two things to keep in mind in triathlon racing – focus on **fun** and foolproof **preparation**. Being fully prepared with your training and race plan will go a long way to allow you to enjoy your race experiences. A failed piece of equipment, chafed skin, or unfamiliarity with the course, for instance, can make for an unpleasant race day. Keep in mind however, that some races may be trials for new strategies, equipment or nutrition elements, and failure may be a part of the learning process to improve for future events.

With your attitude on having a fun experience and learning as many lessons as possible on your race day, you will be motivated to take care of as many details now so they are less problematic during the race weekend. Putting the effort in beforehand will help you succeed on race day. Being able to relax because you are confident you have everything covered will allow you to have more energy for your race, too.

RACE PREPARATION

Make sure you consider every aspect of the race and create your own checklist. A number of checklists and planning charts are included in this chapter to assist you in developing your own "best race prep."

Transitions – One item many forget to prepare for is the transition part of the triathlon. The transition is an important aspect of the race where a lot of time can be made up through planning and practice, particularly for the short races. In the weeks leading up to your key races, be sure to incorporate at least a weekly bike to run "brick," which is a back-to-back workout where you transition from one sport to the next, similar to what you do in a race. This will not only help you rehearse the transition process, but also get you used to the dead leg feeling that often comes from running fast off a hard bike.

A swim-bike brick is also helpful to experience the feeling of going from the swim, where you don't use your legs very much, to the bike, where you may have to push up a hard hill right out of transition and use the leg muscles.

Transition steps to practice include:

- Swim exit gear off (wet suit, goggles)

- T1 gear on (first transition after swim where you put on helmet, cycling shoes, race belt, sunglasses and possibly socks)

- Running with your bike through transition zone and mounting bike at the designated line (there are usually penalties for riding your bike in transition)

- Bike dismount returning to transition zone

- Advanced bike mount and dismount techniques can be developed where you may choose to keep your cycling shoes clipped into your pedals and slip your feet into them after you have mounted you bike in order to save time. Similarly, on the return, you may choose to dismount without unclipping your shoes, which means you must slip your feet out and ride with them on top of your shoes and practice balancing on your shoe, swinging your leg over your saddle, and leaping off to run barefoot back into the transition zone.

- T2 gear exchange (second transition after the bike, where you place your bike on the rack, take off your helmet and slip into running shoes, and possibly a hat and race or fuel belt)

Mental skills practice – This is another area many overlook when preparing for a triathlon. As was discussed in Chapter 6, your mental strength can make or break your race. Preparing your mind by practicing your race-day mantras and self-talk during your tougher training sessions will make it more automatic come race day. If it's raining hard or really windy on the bike, use the arduous weather as a chance to build a calm, strong mind that builds your confidence.

Consider your pre-event rituals and how you prepare your mind best to be focused, calm, positive and mentally tough when faced with challenges. Consider what your mental process will be when faced with a challenging "surprise," like a flat tire or bike crash. If you've already rehearsed the "surprise" in your mind, it will be less stressful and easier to get through.

Nutrition practice – Nutrition is a more important aspect of long distance races such as full and Half-Ironman distance events, and it is very helpful to practice what kind of nutrients, including hydration needs, that you will use on race day. It is never fun during the middle of the race to learn that your favorite peanut butter and jam sandwiches make you ill or that the kind of sugars in a certain sports drink or gel don't agree with your stomach. Pre-race nerves and race day intensity will often make food more difficult to digest, but the more you can test out your nutrition during long training sessions, especially under similar race conditions, the better you will be able to predict your body's needs.

During long training runs or bikes consider measuring your hydration and salt intakes, your sweat rates (by weighing yourself before and after exercise) and recording the temperature/humidity to understand how you are affected.

RACE GOALS
Consider establishing clearly defined goals before you start any race, even if it is as simple as to just have fun, or not walk during the run. A goal will help you keep your mind on your aim, especially through the challenging moments.
• Process goals (skill or mindset mastered)
• Outcome goals (time, pace, or placing)

PRE-RACE PREPARATION CHECKLIST TIMELINES
Week before:
• Make sure your bike is in good working condition
• Make sure you have a good pair of goggles that don't leak
• Decrease your training load, increase or maintain your intensity

Day before:

- Pack your racing bag with swim gear, towel, sunscreen, sunglasses, bike and run gear, and extra clothing and food for after the race. Consider clothing options for various weather scenarios. Pack extra for cold or rainy possibilities. See packing list below.
- Pick up your race packet
- Have your number attached to a number belt or safety pin to your shorts or swimsuit
- Fill water bottles with water and hydration/electrolyte replacements and refrigerate (or freeze if you live in very warm climates) overnight
- Measure out all your race-day nutrition and put in appropriate bags
- Eat and hydrate frequently with normal food and drink. Avoid spicy or heavy foods if you are not used to that, as well as a lot of fiber
- Do some light stretching, yoga and relaxation exercises
- Get to sleep early, but don't worry if you have trouble sleeping as this is common

Race day:

- Wake up around 2-3 hours before the start and eat the foods you are used to having before longer or harder training sessions. Good breakfast foods include a bagel, peanut butter and jam, a banana, applesauce, or smoothies and some form of protein like eggs.
- Arrive at least 1-1.5 hours before the start so you have plenty of time to:
  ◆ park the car
  ◆ get body marked
  ◆ find a good spot in transition if they don't assign it
  ◆ set up your bike
  ◆ hydrate
  ◆ visit the porta-potty
  ◆ check out transition area
  ◆ preview course details if you haven't yet
  ◆ relax and visualize your race plan
  ◆ begin an appropriate warm-up
- Watch you don't get too distracted by the excitement or by other athletes who want to "size up the competition"... always be friendly.

- Review your location in transition. Bring a "special marker" to help you distinguish your spot from others. A colorful towel can catch your attention easily. You can also count the racks so you know exactly where you are as you look for your bike after the swim.
- Get in a warm up. Find a quiet place to stretch, then start with a run, or even a bike if you can take it out of the transition, then get down to the swim start early and get warmed up in the water.
- KNOW THE RULES AND THE COURSE. It is every athlete's responsibility to know the course and the race rules. Have your helmet on AND BUCKLED before you get on your bike and keep it on AND BUCKLED until your bike is racked.
- HAVE FUN! Smile! Finish with a smile or leap!
- Remember to be thankful to volunteers.
- Post-race socializing is fun but don't forget to take care of good post-race nutrition and body care (i.e. ice on a hot day) for optimal recovery.

PACKING CHECKLIST

PRE RACE	SWIM		BIKE	RUN	POST RACE
Sunscreen	Wet suit	☐	Helmet	Run shoes	Warm shirt
Water to sip	Swimsuit	☐	Sunglasses	Run shorts (optional)	Dry undergarments
Towel for transition	Goggles	☐	Fluid bottles	Socks (optional)	Towel for post shower or swim
Music (iPod or walkman)	Extra goggles	☐	Bike shoes	Hat	Warm socks
Extra snack bar in case you get hungry	Swim cap	☐	Bike shorts (optional)		Dry running shoes or sandals
Floor pump to pump up tires pre-race	Extra swim cap	☐	Bike jersey (optional)		Journal
	Body glide	☐	Race belt with number on		Cell phone
			Tools for tire repair (levers, extra tube, CO_2 cartridges, pump)		

RACE PLANS

Consider writing detailed plans for each important aspect of the race:
- Pacing Plan and Course Review
- Nutrition Plan
- Mental Plan

Pacing plan and course review

Before you can know what kind of pacing to plan for, you need to understand the course profile in terms of terrain, elevation changes, and technical sections. Most races will provide route maps online and even elevation profiles. If you do not live near the course to train on it, compare elevation and grade profiles of the course maps to your local terrain. If you have never biked or run the course before, and will not have the chance to do so before you race, at the very least you should drive the course. Knowing the course will help you pace yourself with the appropriate intensity (heart rate, pace per mile or watts power output on a bike). Energy management is especially important for the longer races. Make note of aid station frequency and locations, in order to make decisions on using race aid or your own replenishments.

Course review
☐ Check course maps and outlines on race web site
☐ Ride or drive bike course
☐ Bike or run the run course
☐ Note aid station locations

Pacing Plan
More advanced triathletes will benefit from considering the specific intensity of effort that will be best for them on race day based on their race goals and fitness level. Plan for each discipline too.

	Intensity (heart rate, watts on bike or pace per mile on run)	Perceived effort scale
Warm-up		
Swim		
Bike		
Run		

Nutrition Plan (Key for longer events)

PRE-RACE WEEK PLAN	Mon.	Tues.	Wed.	Thurs.	Fri.
TRAVEL FOOD (to pack)					
GROCERY LIST (to shop for at race site)					

PRE RACE MEALS	Day before:	Morning before:
RACE NUTRITION PLANS	Hydration/electrolytes: (i.e., water, carb fluid, electrolyte tabs) T1 (post swim) – On bike – T2 (post bike) – On run –	Race fuel: (i.e., bars, gels, fruits, snacks) T1 (post swim) – On bike – T2 (post bike) – On run –
CALORIES	Total calories:	Total calories:
CALORIES PER HOUR ESTIMATED		
POST-RACE NUTRITION		

Mental Plan

	Consider worst case scenarios and solutions	Mental skills used
Pre event		Visualizations:
Race day		Relaxation strategies:
Swim		Positive mantras:
T1/T2		Mental approach:
Bike		Positive mantras:
Run		Positive mantras:

POST RACE

- Rinse and hang your wet suit to dry
- Clean and re-lube bike (especially if you raced in the rain or near a saltwater course)
- Write up a brief race report and include your lessons learned to remember for next time. Share with your coach and get feedback if possible
- Write a thank you note to the race director if you had a good time

Post race report and evaluation

Race:
Date:
Evaluation Date:

Goals:	Actual:
Swim	Swim
Bike	Bike
Run	Run
Mental	Mental
Nutrition	Nutrition

Questions to consider:

Were your goals met? Why or why not?

What were 5 positive things about the race for you?

1.

2.

3.

4.

5.

What was your **general feeling** after the race?

How much muscle soreness did you experience after the race?

How was your physical recovery? Slow, fast? What signs of fatigue have you showed?

What do you think your race day strengths were?

What do you think your race day weaknesses were?

What part of your performance do you think you could change most easily?

What do you wish to strive for most in your next performance?

How are you feeling now? Any injuries?

Coach feedback	
Coach race assessment	
Coach guidance for improvement	

RACE TRIPS

Many people make a "vacation" experience out of traveling to a new place or a far-away country to do a triathlon. Find a checklist below to assist your planning for these more complicated races. The extra attention to details will pay off when you can relax and let the trip unfold and be prepared for any difficulties that may arise.

Travel preparations
- Flight details
- Airport transport details
- Car rental or local transportation details
- Passports prepared
- Airline tickets or e-ticket number
- USAT license card (or other triathlon organization card)
- Visas and immunizations (if needed)
- Bike box
- Airline bike waivers (if applicable)

Accommodations
- Hotel address and directions
- Hotel reservation number
- Estimated arrival time and early check in options if needed
- Check-out time

Travel and tour schedules
- Family interests
- Tourist interests

PART 5
Get Balanced

The book concludes with key tips for keeping your sanity while balancing life and triathlon, and delves more deeply into specific challenges for women, such as childcare, menopause, and safety.

CHAPTER 12

BALANCE LIFE AND TRIATHLON

Tri-ing the Juggling Act

So you want to have a life and you want to do triathlon, too?

Triathlon can bring either more chaos and stress or more strength and harmony to your life. It's important to find the balance point between triathlon and other commitments in your life.

The real triathlon challenge can be as much about time management as it is about the swim, bike and run.

Tips for planning and balance:
- Divide up your time for each priority in your life
- Log your training to keep track of how well you are doing
- Plan weekly with specific goals and objectives and review each week
- Have a schedule that meets your objectives, but that is also flexible enough to meet your other commitments and keep the balance
- Find a regular routine that your body will fall into more easily
- Consider less time for commuting and fill it with biking or running to work
- There are only 168 hours in a week – think before you use them!
- Learn from other successfully balanced women

Lydia Delis-Schlosser is a master of time management as a single parent of two teenage sons and a business owner. This didn't stop her from winning the 2004 World Ironman Championships at the age of 45. Ask her what number one time management skill keeps her "together" and successful.

Her response: "The #1 time management skill is integrating my training schedule with my daily calendar, tied in with prepping for workouts the night before ... getting clothes together, fuel prepared. You make your kids' lunches the night before and fill bottles with your training fluids."

It also helps to understand if your goals harmonize with the rest of your life. Do you want to be competitive? Do you want to achieve a goal, like finishing an Ironman? Do you want to just participate and experience a challenge or social opportunities?

For more competitive athletes, like Delis-Schlosser, there often comes a time to consider whether your training is balanced or compulsive. Signs she considers: "When you tell your friends you can't go out drinking on Saturday night because you have a big brick in the morning! Or you go to bed before your kids because you have to get up and do a long run early, and hope they don't stay up all night playing video games!"

Living the triathlon lifestyle

Having a lifestyle approach to triathlon is the healthy way to ensure triathlon stays a beneficial part of your life. Consider how and why the sport brings benefits and balance to your life. Triathlete mom Lydia O'Neil is an example of someone who embraces the triathlon lifestyle with balance and perspective that provides benefit to both her and her family.

Lydia O'Neil – Balancing Act

I work at Dell and do sprint distance triathlons for fun outside of work. I am married with two kids, ages five and six, and my husband also works at Dell. We both do triathlons. My husband did his first full Ironman recently. I have no such ambitions now because I am having enough trouble balancing the career, the kids, etc. as it is. Sprints are fine with me.

I like the triathlons for a few reasons:
1. They help me release stress because they get me out of the house at least four days a week doing something for myself. It is probably the only time of day that I do something exclusively for me, and I think most women are guilty of neglecting themselves because they get too wrapped up in everything else that needs to be done first.
2. I am a happier person when I exercise.
3. I want to set a strong example for my five-year-old daughter that she can be anything she wants to be.
4. Triathlons give me the ability to trade off sports so I am not bored with my workouts.

Getting Creative

Succeeding at fitting in all your daily duties and keeping yourself on track with a training plan can be challenging, especially if you're adding kids and/or a full-time job into the mix. Sandi Wiebe, multiple-time World Champion at both the Olympic and Ironman distance, is a mother of four (the youngest 13 and the oldest 34), grandmother of six, and has relied on getting creative with her situation.

Wiebe shares her story and the ideas that have worked for her to fit in training with the realities of family obligations.

Innovative Irongrandma Sandi Wiebe

Specific to women is the necessity to be creative in fitting in workouts, especially when one has young children. I took up running at age 43 after my fourth child. When I started Ironman training, I had to create workouts with the children in mind. For example, I bought a bike trailer and hauled the kids around. You should have seen the quads I developed pulling 245 pounds (bike, trailer and 2 children included). Things like that – having your kids ride bikes alongside in the park while you run. I bike everywhere I can instead of using a car ,and yes that includes going for groceries, which I think my max has been four bags in the side bags on my mountain bike, rain or shine.

My kids have graduated to bikes of their own but I still ride with my daughter on our tandem – great way to spend time with her. The one thing that I found most useful of all when the kids were young was to make sure that I allotted time for my workout. If you don't, you find the day disappears and by the end of the day, the enthusiasm has also disappeared.

With a family, the day never really has an end (like work in an office) so it's easy for a workout to get lost in the shuffle. In the long run (no pun intended), you feel better if you can do something for yourself as an individual, rather than what is done as "Matthew's mom," etc.

For the past six years, I have taken the kids to school, left the car there and either run or biked home; the reverse at the end of the day for pickup. That way I always got something in. I could decide to either run/bike longer because once I was out, time was the only limitation. My kids got used to the idea after the first few weeks, and I really never cared what the other parents thought about this; I knew what I was doing and accomplishing. Time management is very important when trying to fit in all the day's activities and training. I also work part-time, so it can get hectic at times.

Believe in the power of role models

Many women with children won't give themselves any time because they feel they need to be spending time with children, fulfilling their children's needs and being the "good parent." It is worth a reminder, however, that you can teach your children the most by example, and the happier and healthier you are with more energy to share with them, the more they will appreciate your love as a parent.

Shellie Orosiba's story is a shining example of how your own athletic goals and dreams can positively impact your children.

Orosiba's story should inspire any mom to get out there and tri for her children.

Sometimes I feel guilty because my training time takes me away from my family. I've come to realize, however, that by taking that time, I have more physical strength and energy to deal with my kids (both boys!). Competing in triathlon also teaches me about persistence, commitment and mental strength – things I need to be a better parent.

Until this last year, I did not realize what an impression my efforts in triathlon had made on my older son. Jordan, now 12, has always been a great kid. With that said, he was always the shortest and frailest kid in his class. He was extremely sensitive and burst into tears every time he got the slightest bump or bang. We tried enrolling him in team sports, but he just quit playing when he got tired (which usually didn't take long). In soccer, I think he spent more time on the ground than playing! In baseball, he got hit by the ball once in practice and could never hit another ball again. We always tried to pump him up with positive thoughts ... we tried bribing... we tried threatening. It was embarrassing on the sidelines, but the worst part of it was that my heart just ached for what I could only imagine he must have been going through.

Jordan approached me at the end of last season and advised me he wanted to do triathlon himself. Based on his track record, I was skeptical. How could my fragile child stand up to such a test of endurance and will? I talked to Jordan a lot. I told him about how hard it was. I told him about how I had to push through the pain and be strong mentally. I told him about the preparation. He simply said, "I can do it." I told him I'd have to think about it. After much thought, I came to the realization that he already knew all about what he'd go through because he'd seen me go through it. He'd seen the look of concentration and pain on my face just before I'd crossed over the finish line, and he'd seen the smile come across my face after I'd finished. He'd seen my bloodied legs after a fall on my bike and he'd seen me get right back on and ride. He'd seen my transformation into a triathlete, and he wanted it!

So I said "yes" and set up a training schedule for Jordan about two months ago. He still couldn't swim freestyle (he was always afraid of the water), so we set up two swimming practices a week. I don't know that I'd ever seen Jordan work so hard physically. Over the course of several weeks, he really made a transformation. He flexed his new muscles for me. He swam 200 meters straight in the pool. He transitioned off his bike and into a running sprint! He was proud, and so was I.

Two weeks ago, he did his triathlon race. To be honest, I was a little apprehensive. I didn't want him to quit. I didn't want him to be last. When he lined up with his age-group at the start, he was a full foot shorter than any other kid. At 62 pounds, he only weighed about half of several of the boys! "You can do it, Jordan!" I shouted. I think I was telling it to myself as much as him. Into the water he went. He was slow, but he was steady. Several kids from a later wave started swimming over him. I gritted my teeth. Jordan didn't stop. He kept swimming his nice, slow and steady pace. I expected he was going to be exhausted when he came out of the water. To my surprise and delight, Jordan jumped up out of the water and burst into a full-on sprint. "Go Jordan! Go Jordan!!" He sped out of T1 so quickly he lost his balance and fell onto the street (Gasp!). Jordan hopped back up and darted out onto the bike, seemingly unphased. I waited and waited and waited for him to come back. The faster kids had come in several minutes ago. I started to worry again. Did he get too tired? Did he stop? Did he fall? Then, in the distance, I spotted his shiny red bike. He whirled through T2 and out onto the run. When I saw him approaching the finish, he was flushed ... he his face was grimaced ... and ... he was running fast! When he crossed the line, he leaned over and clutched his sides. He was exhausted! He had given it everything he had!

Jordan didn't come in first, but he wasn't last either. Jordan did something truly amazing that day. He found his inner strength and pushed himself beyond what he (or I, for that matter) thought possible. He was so proud that he refused to wash his race numbers off. In fact, he wore them to school along with his triathlon t-shirt the following Monday. Something in Jordan has changed. He is no longer so much the kid of fear and doubt. He's started learning to play his guitar, he's even talking about joining a swim team, and he's doing another triathlon (of course!). Jordan's accomplishment has empowered him in other aspects of his life!

As a parent, I could never teach Jordan that sense of inner-strength and pride. It was only as a triathlete, that I could show him this ... that he could learn through my own metamorphosis. Not only that, but by my example, Jordan is discovering an active and healthy lifestyle that will make his life longer and fuller. – Shellie Orosiba

CHAPTER 13
OBSTACLES FOR WOMEN IN TRIATHLON

Body respect for health and sanity

The emphasis on appearance is a societal pressure that often forces women to begin triathlon training for the purpose of losing weight and looking better, dreaming of the ideal body with a six pack of abs. I've seen women strive for such goals and when body image takes precedence over inner satisfaction, rarely is there joy and sustainable happiness surrounding their involvement in the sport. There is also added pressure for the more performance-driven athletes with the urge to lose pounds to run faster. Certainly, a lighter physique will be easier to move more swiftly, however, a pre-occupation with eating and body image can be a mindset that is damaging to your overall health.

PRO PERSPECTIVE

I think that most female athletes (at all levels of the sport) lack confidence athletically; we have a different mental skill set than men do. Mental skills to build confidence would be beneficial. Similarly, there is a great focus on body image and weight in the sport that I think leads some women to overtrain and obsess about their training. – Mary Uhl, professional triathlete

Dr. JoAnn Dahlkoetter, sports psychologist and frequent contributor to *Triathlete Magazine* and other publications, writes in her book *Your Performing Edge* some suggested exercises and mental tools that women can employ to empower themselves and build internal acceptance, regardless of body size or shape.

Dr. JoAnn's Exercises for Body Awareness and Respect
(See www.DrJoAnn.com for more info)

Dr. JoAnn suggests closing your eyes, taking 10 deep breaths and asking yourself these questions. Write down your responses and any new insights.
Which part of your body:
• Is the strongest?
• Do you like the best?
• Do people notice first?
• Is most prone to injury?
• Are you most self-conscious about?
• Are you most comfortable with?
Next, pretend that you live outside your body and that someone else could move in. What tips would you give the new occupant about what it's like to be there?
• What kind of care does it need (attention, food, hydration, sunlight, exercise, proper environment, social support, physical affection, healing and recovery)?
• What are its rhythms or routines (hourly, daily, weekly, monthly, seasonally)?

- What tips can you suggest for how to manage this body (knowing when to rest or take an easy training day)?
- How do people respond to this body?

Tools for change and awareness:

- Give yourself healthy living rather than a target, "ideal" weight
- Learn to trust your body and its messages, and adjust to your needs not just your plan
- Keep a log with how your body is feeling every day and use for modifying your plan
- Keep in check with your appetite or hunger levels
- View food as nourishment first, pleasure second
- Reward and nurture yourself

Body Appreciation Training – ask yourself these questions:

- What has my body done for me lately? Think about the wide range of possibilities from:
  - ◆ Become stronger and more flexible
  - ◆ Pulled through a fantastic workout
  - ◆ Healed from injury
  - ◆ Recovered well during sleep
  - ◆ Allowed you to feel enjoyment in life
  - ◆ Helped you achieve an important goal
  - ◆ Learned a new skill
  - ◆ Reached out and made new friends
  - ◆ Created another human being
  - ◆ Learned to relax mentally and physically

Consider your feelings when you write down the answers and review what you appreciate about your body. Remember to allow yourself a few moments each day to reflect and appreciate who you are and what your body has done for you.

Other gender specific differences

Recent research has noted a few differences in the way women swim, bike and run, such as:

- Energy cost is greater for females with shorter arms and that energy cost is also greater for females with a preference for leg use in the front crawl. (Chatard, J.C., Louvie, J.M., Lacour, J.R. [1991] Energy cost of front-crawl swimming in women's. *European Journal of Applied Physiology* 63, 1, 12-16.)

- Female athletes are more likely to have a stroke-rate dominated style of swimming (faster instead of long, gliding strokes).
- Higher body fat increases insulation and buoyancy and may be an advantage to women in ultra swim events.
- For cycling, a women's physique requires different adjustments:
  - ◆ women tend to have wider hips, which means a different saddle and different angle of saddle tilt
  - ◆ women tend to have longer legs (through the thigh) proportionally to their height, which means the saddle will need to be further back and seat angle more shallow
  - ◆ women tend to have a shorter reach and less upper body strength so they need a smaller frame for a reasonable stem length (8-10 cm minimum) to ensure proper bike handling. Many women are put on men's frames and are forced to adjust for the shorter reach with a short stem and forward saddle, which impairs handling and power output.
  - ◆ women are more flexible than men, thus a greater seat-to-bar height can be accommodated
  - ◆ women have smaller feet, which puts them at a mechanical disadvantage and puts more pressure on shin and calf muscles. Women may need shorter cranks (165mm as opposed to the normal 170mm).
- Because of their smaller physical size, women have a higher oxygen requirement per pound of body weight than men, which is a disadvantage on flat time trials.
- Women have a higher ratio of fat to total body weight, which is a disadvantage when climbing hills. Small, slightly built women are more suited to hilly courses over taller, heavier riders best suited for flat courses.
- For running, women are lighter, have smaller feet and wider hips than men. They also have larger breasts that can complicate running.
- Knee problems are more prevalent in women, often due to their wider hips.
- Women pronate more than men. Women should buy running shoes specifically made for women because of their lighter weight,

narrower foot and pronating characteristics. Men's shoes may be too stiff for the lighter woman.
- Women are on average, 10% slower than men at all distances.
- Due to less testosterone production than men, it is more difficult for women in general to build lean muscle mass and women have more subcutaneous fat than men. This accounts for the extra 10% fat on average that women have compared to men.
- The differences between the performances of male and female athletes can be explained most by differences in lean body mass and muscle fiber size. At the elite level, differences in VO_2max can almost all be accounted for by the differences in lean body mass, red blood cell count and physique. Other differences are accounted for by physical (such as gait) and haematological factors (Shangold and Mirkin, 1993).
- Women tend to have smaller hearts than men and higher heart rates at the same level of exertion.This should be considered when using heart rate for training intensity levels.

Similarities between men and women
- Women use the same number of calories per hour of exercise as men (relative to lean body weight)
- Women have similar ratios of Type I and Type II muscle fibers.
- Women produce and clear lactic acid at the same rate as men.

OTHER OBSTACLES

Women experience a few other obstacles due to their unique anatomy, hormones and ability to conceive children.

Gynecological issues – Whether training or not, women can experience discomforts, such as vaginitis, incontinence, menstrual cramps and menopause. Saddle sores are an additional discomfort that develops from cycling.

Vaginitis, yeast infections and saddle sores are best prevented by wearing breathable padded cycling shorts without underwear, and by washing and drying both clothing and body well after each training session. For treatment of any infection, see a physician for appropriate medication. Saddle sores, caused by friction with the bike seat, are eased by ensuring the shorts chamois is clean and dry, that the saddle fits properly and by applying a cream, such as Chamois Cream.

Urinary incontinence will occur in many women when they are running or jumping, especially those women who have given birth several times. Such physical training can cause abdominal pressure and result in involuntary leakage. However,, the situation can be improved by doing specific exercises to help strengthen the pelvic muscles in the area. Pelvic exercises called Kegel exercises have been known to help. The exercises can be done anywhere. Practice by pulling in or "squeezing" your pelvic muscles (as if you are trying to stop urine flow). Hold for about 10 seconds, then rest for 10 seconds. Do 3 to 4 sets of 10 contractions per day. It may take a while to strengthen the muscles so be patient, but most women notice improvement after a few weeks. Making sure the bladder is emptied before training and using a pad can help with this potentially embarrassing problem.

Hormones and menstrual cramps can wreak havoc on a woman's body during menstruation, however, exercise can actually help alleviate symptoms. There is no reason to stop training during menstruation, unless the cramps are severe enough to be debilitating. Many women find some relief to cramp severity by taking a contraceptive pill. There are other benefits to this for athletic women, such as controlling the menstrual cycle to be in line with the training and competition cycle.

The cessation of menstruation as women age changes hormones and results in menopause, which most commonly occurs in the mid-fifties. Many of the symptoms associated with menopause, such as sleeplessness and depression, can be alleviated with physical training so it should not be avoided during this time. In fact, due to the loss of bone density and increased risk of osteoporosis during this period, weight-bearing exercise, along with vitamin and nutritional supplementation, is extremely beneficial. Physical activity can help lower cholesterol levels, which tend to increase after menopause.

Emily Bruno, a nurse and extraordinary masters triathlete, writes about the menopause experience in her book *Ironwomen Never Rust: Making Memories While Managing Menopause.*

Pregnancy – This is a special time in a woman's life when training needs to be modified, but not eliminated (unless you have complications and have been advised by your physician to limit physical activity). There are many women who continue running, and even do a marathon or triathlon, while pregnant. However, given the dramatic needs of the body for developing a child, the intensity of training and racing needs to be reduced to healthy, unstressful levels. It is most wise to consult closely with a physician to get clearance to exercise during pregnancy. Consider keeping the heart rate lower if you are used to challenging speed sessions. Riding a bike can also be dangerous due to the possibility of a collision or falling off the bike, so it is wise to consider the safety of the situation.

Also, exercise during pregnancy and nursing requires extra support in clothing. Mothers in Motion makes a great line of technical clothing for exercising moms-to-be, including shorts that have a neoprene liner to support your baby belly. Also, if you run during pregnancy, you will need very frequent bathroom stops. So it is best to plan runs close to appropriate facilities.

Terry Ziehr, triathlon mother of three

"When I was pregnant, I trained but at lower intensities. I remember running a 5k race in my eighth month with Jacob and passing people. To me, my nine months were a bit of a break from training. I did a lot of walking and tried to get a lot of rest with good nutrition. It's nice to think that as a woman we can do anything and be 'super' all the time, but pregnancy is a special time. There will always be another marathon or race to run when you're not pregnant. I think that Yoga and low impact sports, like swimming, are great. Pregnancy is a wonderful time to slow things down a bit and just love that little miracle within."

For more resources on this topic, consider reviewing books, such as *Exercising Through Your Pregnancy*, by Dr. James Clapp, and *Runner's World Guide to Running and Pregnancy* by Chris Lundgren.

Childcare issues – Finding time to train for triathlon while you are also putting energy into raising your children can no doubt be a challenge. However, the healthier and fitter you are, the more strength and energy you will have to help take care of them and participate in activities with them. Parental endurance and stamina can be trained for through your own physical activities. Also your mental outlook can be enhanced after you get out to do your own workout. Giving yourself your own goals and sticking to your training regimen can allow you to have more peace of mind and patience in dealing with the everyday stresses of raising children.

As was discussed more thoroughly in Chapter 12, creative solutions are needed to harmoniously incorporate triathlon training and races with the needs of your growing family. Many mothers take advantage of childcare at gyms, trade care-taking time with other mothers, or use friends and family to look after younger children while doing their own swim, bike or run. When the kids are old enough, they can join mom for the workout in a baby jogger or bike trailer. When they get even older, they can accompany mom during the workout by biking alongside while she runs or participate in their own swim class while mom does her swim workout. Moms can also take advantage of "sideline" time at soccer or baseball games by doing a run around the field or setting up a bike trainer to put in a few miles while cheering her kids on the field.

Kids love to be active and learn. See what creative ways you can get them to be included so they don't feel excluded from your "selfish" training. They may enjoy trying a few yoga poses, filling your water bottles or helping map out the miles on your next long bike ride.

Safety issues – There are always risks in every activity you choose to do. Women need to be aware of the risks and avoid situations or take precautions to reduce those risks. Here are a few tips to prepare yourself to bike or run safely:

- Check in with the local police department to inquire about incidents reported for your running and biking area.

- Devise "safe" running and cycling– take a look at maps and tell others your route if going alone. Consider the light situation if you run early, at night or dusk.
- Carry some form of ID. A great product called Road ID can be worn on your shoe or ankle while running. Also include in your ID system any allergies or medical issues in case of an accident and you are unable to advise emergency medical assistants.
- Consider carrying a personal alarm or pepper spray to scare off a potential attacker.
- Be prepared for dangerous animals – such as dogs, or depending on part of the world you live in, you could be at risk for bear attacks in the wilderness, and/or bobcat or mountain lions on mountain trails.

CHAPTER 14
GET IN THE GAME
By special guest writer Cherie Gruenfeld

In fitting form, the final chapter of this book is written by triathlon legend Cherie Gruenfeld, a six-time World Ironman Age-Group Champion and founder of a non-profit program called Exceeding Expectations that uses triathlon to help at-risk, inner-city kids in San Bernardino, California.

Like me, Cherie is clearly a woman who loves to be in the game. Throughout the spring of 2006 we exchanged multiple emails as we were both coming back from exercise layoffs. We would encourage each other and celebrate each longer workout and little physical victory we were making. Coming back from a long period of inactivity is not easy and I could use all the help I could get. At the end of May, she wrote to say her training for Ironman Coeur D'Alene was completely derailed. A bike accident had left her with a broken sacrum and damaged her shoulder beyond use. She was clearly out of the game.

At that point, I was struggling to finish my book. I needed help staying in the writing game, so I suggested Cherie help write a chapter for my book to help me and to help her keep her mind off of her unfortunate plight. Graciously, she agreed. The result is the final message of my book, persuasively written to encourage women to take what they have learned in the previous chapters to "Get it Together," "Get Moving," "Get Involved," "Get Training," "Get Balanced" and make the final leap to 'Get in the Game.' – *Lisa Lynam*

"It is not the critic who counts, nor the one who points out how the strong man stumbled or how the doer of deeds might have done them better. The credit belongs to the man who is actually in the arena; whose face is marred with sweat, dust and blood; who strives valiantly; who errs and comes home again and again; who knows the great enthusiasms, the great devotions and spends himself in a worthy cause and who, if he fails at least fails while bearing greatly so that his place shall never be with those cold and timid souls who know neither victory nor defeat."

Theodore Roosevelt

After nearly 15 years in the sport of triathlon, I have come to believe that the biggest risk to woman is that they never try, but rather sit on the sidelines feeling this is something that is beyond them.

I've spoken with countless women watching their husbands or kids participate, but when the topic of doing a triathlon comes up, they wave it away, almost automatically. "Those people out there are different than me".

And they're right. The difference is that these people are out there doing it. But many of them used to be spectators, as well. Then someone came along, pointed to the finish line and said, "Yes … you can". And they believed it, and now they're doing it. They are in the arena.

Triathlon is a relatively new sport, so many of us lucky enough to be involved feel a personal responsibility to help other women get involved. Sally Edwards, a well-known women's triathlete advocate, says it best: "We must help them find the inner athlete in themselves."

What makes a woman stand back, afraid to take the risk?

Based on my experience as a female, a triathlete and a coach, I have a few thoughts on the subject that I hope will help you take that first step.

Is it "all about me?"

Even in today's world of increasing equality, it's still not unusual for a woman to feel that she simply doesn't have the right to indulge herself in a demanding pursuit, such as triathlon. She may feel that getting involved in a sport such as triathlon, where so much time and dedication are required, is a luxury not available to her while she is still basically responsible for the household and child rearing.

This issue of triathlon being self-indulgent for a woman is one that should be put to rest. The female triathletes who have spoken throughout these pages have certainly found lives that fulfill their needs as well as those of their families. In fact, many cope with their family responsibilities even better because they are happy and fulfilled, taking on and accomplishing personal goals. Training for triathlons is a time and energy-consuming venture. It has an impact (positive or negative) on those who depend upon you. I'm not a trained psychologist, but I have, on more occasions than I can count, seen the family's pride when Mom crosses the finish line, and I know enough to understand that this accomplishment has changed her in ways that will benefit everyone around her. Women *belong* "in the arena".

What a fool!

Who among us, man or woman, is comfortable embracing a challenge where we appear to be a total novice and look foolish? If you haven't been on a bike since childhood, have never been a runner or will have to use the breaststroke to make the swim distance, the chance of looking foolish at some point is pretty good. But as long as others are in the same boat, who cares?

One of the best ways to ease into triathlon is through an all-women race, such as the Danskin or Reebok series. These races are designed to address many of the issues mentioned above. You'll race with a group of women, most of them novices, who come from varying backgrounds, all ages and many different sizes and shapes. The one thing you'll all have in common is the desire to take the challenge and have a good time. No one will notice or care when you make a mistake. Everyone is exposing herself and making mistakes. It's an opportunity to learn and laugh at yourself in the process.

Danskin spokeswoman Sally Edwards promises to be the last one to cross the finish line. If coming in dead last is a fear you secretly harbor, relax. It simply cannot happen. This is your chance to be a player and find your inner athlete.

The men in our lives

My experience has been that most men are extremely supportive of women in sports. Regretfully, however, there are a few men left in this new age who still have trouble with this concept. In some relationships, the woman knows that it will be an issue at home if she should happen to perform better than her husband/boyfriend.

In the All-Women races, you have no chance of over-shadowing the male in your life since he won't be on the race course with you. Hopefully, he'll be there to watch you and will find himself part of a large group of men, each supporting his own particular woman. With luck, this will start a new pattern and when you progress to participating in "co-ed" triathlons, he'll support you and will feel pride in seeing you in the arena.

Is my butt hanging out?

Although I think we've gotten over the belief that the ideal body is the one we see in the pages of fashion magazines, we all still have parts and pieces that we'd exchange in a heartbeat. Many of us have, since early childhood, learned what to wear to hide or at least disguise those areas. In a triathlon, however, there's nowhere to hide. In order to swim, bike and run, we're going to have to take it nearly all off and let the world see what we've been so protective of all these years.

In 1996, Judy Molnar helped break down that barrier for us. While sitting in the doctor's office, Judy glanced at her medical file and read the phrase "morbidly obese." Those two words changed Judy's life, and she has since gone on to change the lives of many other women.

She realized she wanted to live, needed to be healthy to do that and the road she took was becoming a triathlete. Judy, now a strong, healthy woman, shed many, many pounds and participated twice in the Ironman World Championships in Kona.

Look around you at any race and you'll see a multitude of different bodies, some great, some not so great. When you're sitting on the sidelines and see a woman race by who might not have the tight little butt of a twenty-year-old, my guess is that you didn't spend one moment thinking about her butt, but rather your thoughts run more along the lines of: "Wow, isn't it great that she's out there doing it!"

Well, that could be you.

It makes no difference what's flopping around or hanging out. Believe me, nobody cares. What matters is crossing the finish line, a victor in every sense of the word.

Won't I hurt myself?

As I sit here, my arm is in a sling and I'm sitting on a pillow protecting a fractured hip. This would not have happened to me had I not been riding my bike. Triathlon is a risky sport. Nobody enjoys being injured, but it comes with the territory. Men who played sports growing up learned that getting hurt is part of being active, but women have only recently become exposed to injury as they've gotten more involved in keeping fit. Jumping into the world of triathlon seems to be taking the risk of injury to another level.

One could easily see this risk of injury as a good reason (or excuse) not to get involved. It is true that, if you play, you will at some time be down with an injury. But I can personally vouch for the fact that being inactive comes with its own set of aches and pains and long-term debilitating effects. A broken bone or a pulled hamstring will heal. The physical and mental effect of inactivity will last a lifetime. Be smart and cautious, but don't let the possibility of injury make you fearful and keep you on the sidelines.

Injuries happen

An injury, such as a sprained ankle or a broken collarbone suffered in a bike crash, can occur at any time, even while following the healthiest training program. Some athletes actually invite trouble when they start to feel that more is better and fall into the overtraining trap. Regardless of how it happened, when it does, it's time to look for an approach that is effective in healing, mentally and physically, and to get back into the game as quickly as possible. The physical side is dependent on the injury, but here are a few ideas for the mental side of healing, which is really all about *handling downtime productively*.

- Take some time away from the activity that caused the problem. Allow yourself plenty of time rather than testing the injury every day or setting a hard and fast timetable for a return to full training. Replace training time with other activities that you enjoy and will keep you active.
- Happiness is having something to look forward to, even if it's 12-18 months away. Set a new race goal, but be realistic. Give yourself plenty of time so that you don't have to rush the comeback.
- Refocus on activities that you tend to neglect when training full-time. Stay productive. Set new goals in non-physical areas. Try to learn a new skill. Re-establish old friendships that you may have let fall by the wayside while focusing on your training.
- Get involved with something where you can work with other people, helping them in some way. There's no better way to get your mind off yourself and your troubles than to get involved with people or projects where your full attention is required.
- Keep structure in your life. For example, the routine of the alarm clock starting your day will help you feel a purpose to your life and the day ahead.
- Maintain some fitness with workouts that use uninjured parts of your body. If you're nursing a cranky hamstring, swim with pull buoys, which will protect your hamstring while working your upper body.
- Don't let your healthy diet fall apart. Continued good nutrition will help hasten the physical healing and will keep you feeling good, contributing to your mental well-being. When you find yourself picking up extra weight, the most common reaction is eating while

you complain about your body changing shape. This won't take you in the right direction.

- Don't be afraid to let others help you. We've all been there and we've found our way out. Let us guide you.

*   *   *

Female health issues

I have tried to address those issues that might make a woman stand on the sidelines rather than take a chance and get into the game. If I've been successful, and you are ready to take the leap and become part of this multisport community: Welcome!

At this point, you ought to be aware of certain challenges that female triathletes face to some degree, at one time or another. Finding ways to work around them is what gets us where we want to go.

The female athlete triad

Eating disorders, amenorrhea (lack of a menstrual cycle) and osteoporosis make up the "triad" associated with female athletes, young and old, and can become a downward spiral very quickly. Body image becomes the focus, no monthly periods seem like a blessing and a stress fracture is the next thing to follow. The woman who falls prey to the triad may very likely deny the pain and keep training, in order to keep the body she wants. At this point she's risking a complete break of the bone, which is becoming brittle with osteoporosis. You can't out-run this.

The first order of business is to get the periods started again. Your gynecologist, after scolding you for letting it go on, will help you get your body back into its normal cycle, which is necessary for maintaining healthy bones.

Your doctor may recommend a bone-density test, a procedure that will let you know if you're at risk for osteoporosis. The doctor can then make specific recommendations for life-style changes that can help you stay healthy as you continue your athletic life.

The female cycle

Every young woman in the sport will face the issue of training and racing through menstrual cramps and bleeding. Later on, the possible effects of the hormonal changes of menopause or hormone replacement therapy (HRT) may kick in. No two women will react to these things in exactly the same way, so the effect of these changes on performance are not easily predicted nor is there a single answer to the problem. Menstruation is more easily managed because it is better understood whereas menopause can severely hamper one woman while another hardly knows it's going on. Unfortunately, medical professionals of today are of little help in explaining why. The best advice, I believe, is to be forewarned. Know that there may be times when your performance is sub-par and the only explanation is that you're a woman. (A small price to pay for the gift of children.)

*   *   *

The woman triathlete – in the arena

It's no secret that there are differences between men and women. But, by and large, in the world of triathlon, the differences are minimal. For every unique discomfort or health issue we females encounter, men will have one of their own. While your bike seat is horribly uncomfortable, his may not only be uncomfortable but may be causing serious medical problems. When some women with large breasts are putting on a second bra for comfort while running, men are taping their nipples to keep them from chafing while they run. We all get saddle sores and chlorine-damaged hair and occasionally suffer from dehydration and hyponatremia.

Where we do differ is in our late entry into the sport, in large numbers. It's important for women to realize that the world of multisport is available and to know that females all over the world have found triathlon to be a playing field for them, one where they can excel. Women today have opportunities only dreamed of a generation ago. The risk is not that we perform poorly or that we get hurt. The risk is that we fail to try; that we spend our lives saying, "I think I could have" or "I wish I had."

The game is afoot. Come join us "in the arena."

RESOURCES

Women's triathlon web sites

www.active.com/activewomen
– online fitness site with event registration and resources for women

www.hertri.info
– online calendar of women only triathlons

www.hersports.com
– a magazine for women who want to lead a healthier, more active lifestyle. For real women who like to run, bike, hike, ski.

www.irongirl.com
– web site for Irongirl events, apparel and resources

www.jamtrisuits.com
– trisuits for women designed by women

www.momsinmotion.com
– fitness programs for women to prepare for an event based on fun and philanthropy

www.ontri.com
– online community for triathletes, including a women's club section

www.trinewbies.com
– web site for beginner with a women-only section

www.teamenvision.com
– all-women's triathlon team based in Boston

www.trichic.com
– online site for dedicated female age-group triathletes with discounts for team members

www.womenstriclub.com
– club for women triathletes, info on women-only races

Women's Triathlon related books

A Female Cyclist, by Gale Bernhardt
A Woman's Guide to Bikes and Biking, by Julie Harrell
A Woman's Guide to Cycling, by Susan Weaver
Caterpillars to Butterflies, by Triathletes from the Danskin Women's Triathlon Series*, Sally Edwards, Maggie Sullivan
Ironwomen Never Rust, by Emily Bruno
Paula Newby Fraser's Peak Fitness for Women, by Paula Newby Fraser
Runner's World Complete Book of Women's Running, by Dagny Scott
Running and Walking for Women Over Forty, by Kathrine Switzer
The Triathlete's Guide to Mental Training, by Jim Taylor and Terri Schneider
The Triathlete's Guide to Bike Training, by Lynda Wallenfels
The Triathlete's Guide to Off-season Training, by Karen Buxton
The Woman Triathlete, by Christina Gandolfo
Triathlons for Women, 3rd Edition, by Sally Edwards

Life books for women

Drop the Juggling Act: Achieve Life Balance, by Connie Herman, Ph.D., and CEO of Strategic Learning Inc. (SLI)

Flex Time: A Working Mother's Guide to Balancing Career and Family, by Jacqueline Foley

From Burned out to Fired up: A women's guide to Rekindling the Passion and Meaning in Work and Life, by Leslie Goodwin

The Hurried Woman Syndrome: A Seven-Step Program to Conquer Fatigue, Control Weight, and Restore Passion to Your Relationship, by Brent W. Bost

The Third Shift: Managing Hard Choices in Our Careers, Homes, and Lives as Women, by Michele Kremen Bolton

The Working Woman's Guide to Managing Stress, by J. Robin Powell, Holly George-Warren

COACHES

See www.usatwomen.com to find a list of clinics and women coaches supporting women specific training programs. Below is a partial list of women who belong to the Women's Commission and offer clinics or programs for women specifically. This is a partial list only – there are many more women out there so it is not all-inclusive. But it might provide a start for your local area.

Partial list of U.S. Women who coach and conduct triathlon clinics and belong to the USAT Women's Commission

Name	Location	Specialty	Contact info
Anthony, Amber D.	San Antonio, TX	USAT Level I Coach, WC Co-Vice Chair of Membership, WC Camps and Clinics Committee	www.rungearrun.com
Brode, Staci	Dallas, TX	Triathlon Coach, Playtri Coaching, Camps and Races	staci@playtri.com (214) 405-5092 www.playtri.com

Name	Location	Specialty	Contact info
Callahan, Celeste	Denver, CO	USAT Level II Coach, Founder and Head of Team CWW Triathlon with an annual membership of 285, full-time volunteer coach	www.cww-triathlon.org/
Claycomb, Kierstyn	Boston, MA	Scientist, Public Relations & Outreach Coordinator for Team Envision, a Boston-based all-women's triathlon team.	kiersie@msn.com www.teamenvision.com
Cleere, Michelle, M.A., NASM, USAT	444 62nd St Oakland, CA	Sports Psychology Consultant	womenwhotri@aol.com 415-860-9517
Donaldson, Joyce	Sylvania, OH	USAT Official, Race Directors Commission USAT (1999-present), Secretary USAT Mideast Regional Federation (IL, IN, KY, MI, OH), Troy Jacobson Academy Coach 2000, USAT Level I Coach	www.eliteendeavors.com
Donovan, Peggy	Grandview, MO	Triathlon Coach, Director, Triathlon 101 and 102 Clinics	tri101coach@aol.com
Jankowitz, Susan	Sparta, NJ	USCF Club Coach	www.spartatech.com
LeMair, Tzatzil	Austin, TX	Founder of TCDC Fitness, Inc. (Tough Cookies Don't Crumble!), a women's multisport training company and producer of the Tough Cookie	tzatzil@tcdcfitness.com www.toughcookies.com

Name	Location	Specialty	Contact info
		Women's Duathlon, USAT Level I Coach, USA Cycling Level 3 coach	
Nenninger, Ina	Vienna, VA		www.triitnow.com
Nielsen, Preben	Chico, CA	Fitness Expert and Director of Triathlon programs for Women	www.womenstriclub.com
Schanbacker, Sharon	Doylestown, PA	AAFA Certified Fitness Trainer/Personal Trainer, Mentor for beginning/ advanced runners, Triathlon Coach/Mentor for TriNewbies, active Community Leader (for primarily fitness activities)	hsssh@comcast.net
Schneidewind, Renee	Chicago, IL	Owner of Max Multisport Training, USAT Level 1 Coach, Personal Trainer	renee@maxmultisport.com
Scott, Victoria	Seattle, WA	President, Body Electric Fitness Co., USAT Level I Coach,	www.bodyelectricfitness.com
Skiles, Kris	Boulder, CO	USAT Level I coach, NASM Certified Personal Trainer, Wellness Consultant, 24 years in triathlon, Course Coordinator for the Boulder Peak Kid's Triathlon	kskiles1@msn.com

Photo Credits

Trevor Hall (pp. 77, 95, 106)
Caroline Yee (p. 85)
Conrad Young (p. 120)

All other photos by Bakke-Svensson/WTC or from private archives

Cover design: Jens Vogelsang

Coverphotos: Robert Oliver, Bakke-Svensson/WTC